Teaching Phonemic Awareness through Children's Literature and Experiences

Teaching Phonemic Awareness through Children's Literature and Experiences

Ɒ

NANCY ALLEN JURENKA, ED.D.

Teacher Ideas Press, an imprint of Libraries Unlimited

Westport, Connecticut • London

Library of Congress Cataloging-in-Publication Data

Jurenka, Nancy E. Allen, 1937-
      Teaching phonemic awareness through children's literature and experiences / by Nancy
Allen Jrenka.
            p.   cm
      Includes index.
      ISBN: 1–59469–000–6 (pbk.)
            1. English language—Phonemics—Study and teaching—United States.   2. Reading—Phonetic method—
United States.   3. School children—Books and reading—United States.   I. Title.
      LB1050.34.J87   2005
      372.46'5—dc22   2005044279

British Library Cataloguing in Publication Data is available.

Library of Congress Catalog Card Number: 2005044279
ISBN: 1-59469-000-6

First published in 2005

Libraries Unlimited/Teacher Ideas Press, 88 Post Road West, Westport, CT 06881
A Member of the Greenwood Publishing Group, Inc.
www.lu.com

Printed in the United States of America

The paper used in this book complies with the
Permanent Paper Standard issued by the National
Information Standards Organization (Z39.48–1984).

10   9   8   7   6   5   4   3   2   1

Contents

Acknowledgments

Teaching Phonemic Awareness through Children's Literature and Experiences resulted from help and information from many people. Central Washington University colleagues and students, as well as friends, provided me with much-appreciated advice and information. The librarians at the public libraries of King County, Bellevue, Washington, Ellensburg, Washington, and Corvallis, Oregon, provided valuable help and interest. A special thank you goes to Becky Poblete for book search assistance and to Paulette Louis and Andrea Sledge for technical assistance. Jane at Lilypad Books in Issaquah, Washington, generously provided me with many helpful suggestions. For support and enouragement, sharp-eyed editing, and wise suggestions for improvement, I am grateful to Suzanne Barchers.

Introduction

The purpose of *Teaching Phonemic Awareness through Children's Literature and Experiences* is to nurture literacy development through weaving together children's picture books read aloud, phonemic awareness activities, experience-based chart stories, letter identification activities, play with language, and poetry. When developing reading and writing skills and strategies, teachers and parents need a many-faceted approach that incorporates all features of language.

The definition of reading that guided the book's creation may be summed up as: Reading/ writing is an active language using process during which the reader/writer uses information coming from the reader's experience, the graphophonic cueing system (sound/letter association), syntactic cueing system (sentence structure and grammar), and semantic cueing system (meaning) in order to construct meaningful text.

THE COMPONENTS

Teaching Phonemic Awareness through Children's Literature and Experiences consists of thirty lessons, one each for all the initial consonants, excluding "X" but including both hard and soft "C" and "G." In addition, there are lessons for the long and short vowels—a, e, i, o, u.

Each lesson consists of nine components described in detail below:

1. Read Aloud

2. Read Aloud to Emphasize the Sound of the Letter

3. Experience-based Chart Story

4. Sound of the Letter Activity

5. Letter Identification Activity

6. Play with Language

7. Poem

8. Supplementary Books

9. Your Ideas

Read Aloud

In the Read Aloud component, a picture book that features the targeted letter is presented to the children. In this manner the children are introduced to a letter and its sound within the context of intact, whole language.

Why read aloud? From an educator's point of view, reading aloud picture books is a proven and highly effective instructional strategy. Reading aloud supports the teaching of a child's concept of story, development of literary appreciation, the sharpening of awareness of the elements of design, and introducing literary elements.

From the child's point of view, listening to a picture book read aloud is fun. Fun is the currency of childhood. It is no small thing to children. The task of the emergent reading teacher is to sell children on the joy and pleasure of reading. Reading aloud well-illustrated picture books brings the world of enjoyment, imagination, and story into the child's hands, eyes, mind, and ears with an immediacy unmatched by other media. Once introduced to a picture book during the read-aloud time, a child can return to a well-loved picture book again and again. Picture books are never to be forgotten friends.

Picture books for young children often capture the cadence and rhythm of language. The well-written picture book begs to be read aloud because children respond to the musical qualities of language. Picture book authors and illustrators are among the most imaginative and creative talents among us. In cooperation with their editors, they produce books that delight and enchant readers. When a charming, humorous picture book such as *Possum Come a-Knockin'* by Nancy Van Laan, illustrated by George Booth, is read aloud with a touch of verve and theatrics, the listening child is captivated.

Read-aloud guidelines include:

- Practice, practice, practice. Reading aloud to an audience of children is, after all, theater and it deserves rehearsal. This is a wonderful opportunity for you to be silly and emphasize the book's humor. It takes practice to get your tongue around the bouncy, playful lines of *Bubble Gum, Bubble Gum* by Lisa Wheeler.

- Check on the pronunciation of words, especially if they are in a language other than your own, as was the case for me with "Onigashima" in Judy Sierra's *Tasty Baby Belly Buttons.*

- Introduce the book. Offer a few clues about the content and for what the children should be listening. The first time the book is read, emphasize the content. The second time the book is read, have the children listen for a targeted sound of a letter.

- Share the illustrations. Practice reading the book so that the children may see the illustrations. Pause to allow them to enjoy the humor. For example, give them time to giggle over Kevin O'Malley's *Leo Cockroach . . . Toy Tester.* Often the illustrations are telling one story, maybe even two or three, while the text is telling another. In Steven Kellogg's *Penguin Pup for Pinkerton,* the main story line is embedded in the dialogue between Emily and the other story characters. The Pinkerton illustrations carry the story line of his caring for his "penguin egg" as well as his inner thoughts and dreams. Rose, the cat, has her own story to tell, as revealed by cartoon balloons. Be sure the children catch all the stories going on in the picture book.

- Be enthusiastic. A primary goal of teachers and parents who wish to nurture children's literacy development is bonding children with books. Enthusiasm is contagious and one of the best tricks of the teaching trade for achieving this goal.

- Ham it up. When reading aloud *I Stink* by Kate and Jim McMullan, get into the role of the garbage truck. It is a perfect book for men to read to young children. Children get a big kick out of hearing guys reading this book with proper sound effects.

- Invite interaction. Have the children interact with and respond to the picture book. They love to repeat chants and repeated lines spontaneously. They like to chime in and make predictions.

- Keep the read-aloud experience happy and short. Quit before children become restless. Stop while they are asking for more.

- Add variety. In addition to the books suggested in the text, find picture books that put a strong emphasis on rhythm, as for example, Steve Webb's *Tanka Tanka Skunk*. Another type of picture book to use is one such as *Baloney* by Jon Scieszka, illustrated by Lane Smith. With its use of interspersed nonsense words, it is a perfect vehicle for modeling how to use context. Picture books that illustrate songs enchant, entertain, and educate. Have fun singing along enthusiastically with the children. Later on, the familiarity of the songs will support the children as they begin to navigate the written text. Some suggestions for songs turned into picture books are:

Fitzgerald, Ella, & Van Alexander. 2003. *A Tisket, a Tasket.* Illustrated by Ora Eitan. New York: Philomel Books.
Raffi. 2004. *This Little Light of Mine.* Illustrated by Stacey Schuett. New York: Alfred A. Knopf.
Shulman, Lisa. 2002. *Old MacDonald Had a Workshop.* Illustrated by Ashley Wolff. New York: G. P. Putnam's Sons.

Perhaps a teacher's first duty is to enchant. With that in mind, humor and fun are primary elements in *Teaching Phonemic Awareness through Children's Literature and Experiences.* The picture books in this collection range from heartwarming to zany. All will bring a smile at the very least and at the most, riotous laughter. All were chosen to enchant. The criteria used to identify the books to be read aloud were:

- Enchantment quality.

- How clearly the targeted letter is used in the text.

- Humor. The text needed to reflect some amount of amusing quality.

- Attractive illustrations. The books were all judged on appealing illustrations that worked well with the text.

- The read-aloud potential. Most picture books in this book were selected for their quality of being read aloud. Often they were described as "begs to be read aloud."

- Educational value. The children listening to the book will learn something new from the book's content, hear lively language, and/or be introduced to literary elements.

- Potential to lead to an experiential response related to the targeted letter as well as, in most cases, the book's content.

Picture books fascinate and intrigue. Watch a child totally absorbed by the beauty of *The Rainbow Fish,* tracing with her fingers the illustrations lines or giggling at Janet Steven's comedic drawings in *Cook-a-Doodle-Doo!* The illustrator's devices work to capture a giggle, a smile, a sigh, a comprehending.

Reading aloud a well-illustrated picture book written with flair by a skilled author is a surefire combination to lead children to the delight of reading. When the author, the illustrator, and the teacher/reader have all done their work, children practically leap out of their seats with enthusiasm. They giggle. They gasp. They participate. They beg for the story to be read again and again.

Read Aloud to Emphasize the Sound of the Letter

In this lesson component the picture book is read aloud a second time in order to heighten the child's awareness of the sound of the targeted letter, an instructional strategy to develop phonemic awareness. Research has shown that developing phonemic awareness is a critical component in instructional programs for emergent readers (Snow, Burns, & Griffin, 1998; Cunningham, Cunningham, Hoffman, & Yopp, 1998).

As the books are read aloud a second time to emphasize the sound of the targeted letter, it is suggested that the reader use a technique known as *rubber banding* (Fox, 2004, p. 42). This technique involves stretching a word so that children may more easily hear the separate sounds. Teachers using this technique distribute rubber bands for the children to stretch as they hear the sounds drawn out. Some words lend themselves to this technique better than others. For example, "man" is easily stretched to "mmmmaaaaannnnn" but "Dan" is not. A word such as "Dan" is pronounced with a heavy emphasis on the initial consonant followed separately by the remainder of the word so that it is pronounced "/D/ -aaannn/."

Phonemic awareness has been shown to be basic to a child's ability to use the graphophonic cueing system to recognize words (Cunningham, Cunningham, Hoffman, & Yopp, 1998). In *Teaching Phonemic Awareness through Children's Literature and Experiences,* phonemic awareness is being developed within the meaningful context of a picture book. Phonemic awareness is one of several basic elements of language, along with syntax, semantics, and experiences, that readers use during the reading process. Phonemic awareness consists of the ability to recognize the isolated sounds within a word, to be able to rhyme, to be able to blend sounds into words. Most children acquire skill with phonemic awareness in a natural manner as parents and teachers read to them and engage children in language play. Eighty percent of first graders have acquired phonemic awareness by the middle of first grade (Vacca, Vacca, Gove, Burkey, Lenhart, & McKeon, 2003, p. 121). "About one out of four middle-class children will have difficulty with phonological awareness unless he or she is given a program of systematic instruction" (Gunning, 2000, p. 3). While phonemic awareness is essential, it is also important to teach it within the context of enchanting picture books, language experience stories, and playing with language activities. It is critical not to lose a child's love for story with repeated use of dreary paper and pencil lessons.

Experience-based Chart Story

In the Experience-based Chart Story component, a language experience approach is employed. Fresh as next Monday morning and as time-honored as school itself, language experience is a proven effective literacy instructional strategy (Hall, 1978; Lee & Allen, 1963; Stauffer, 1970; Tompkins, 2003). Language experience is especially useful with emergent readers and writers. In describing language experience, Reutzel and Cooter state, "As young children are initially challenged by the transcription demands when writing, many teachers turn to a long practiced and very useful early writing" (Reutzel & Cooter, 2004, p. 396).

Experience-based chart stories have several advantages. The language belongs to the child. The word choice and sentence structure are the child's, thus creating a text that is familiar, natural, and highly predictable. Because the recounting is in the child's own language, the child feels ownership of the story and this creates an ongoing desire to read. As a chart story is written by the adult, the child also experiences conventions of language. He or she sees that language moves from left to right and from top to bottom. The child observes that words have spaces between them. An experience-based chart story helps children to see that written language is constructed out of oral language.

In this component the experience piece is emphasized. If reading and writing are to be meaningful, these skills and strategies must be grounded in experiences. Reading and writing are experience-based. Experience is foundational to vocabulary and meaning development as well as to recognizing letter sound relationships. It is out of experiences that the number of words in a child's oral language repertoire emerges and increases. Oral language strength in turn supports phonemic awareness, letter sound associations, vocabulary development, and comprehension. "The most predictable text for a child to begin reading is a text transcribed from her oral dictation of a personally meaningful event or experience" (Reutzel & Cooter, 1996, p. 173).

In *Teaching Phonemic Awareness through Children's Literature and Experiences,* the experiences are ways to respond to the content of the book and/or the targeted letter and its sound. For example, in the "W" lesson that is based on *A Red Wagon Year* by Kathi Appelt, the children gather old toys and books, form a wagon parade, and deliver these items to a class of younger children. After the delivery is made, the children gather in front of chart paper and recount what occurred to the teacher.

In addition or as an alternative to chart stories, the teacher/parent may wish to encourage children to write scribble stories. Scribble stories are stories in the form of scribbled lines written by young children. Some children write scribble stories naturally, on their own; some need permission to write scribble stories; still other children need to be shown how and encouraged to write in this manner. Early in the scribble story writing process, an adult may write in manuscript writing the child's dictation of his or her scribble story underneath the scribble sentences. As a letter is introduced, the children may be encouraged to write the letter where it occurs in the scribble story. As letters are learned and used, scribble stories evolve into phonetic renditions of the children's speech. Eventually, the children will write an entire story in a combination of conventional and phonetic (sometimes referred to as *invented*) spelling. The text constructed from the child's experience can become the source for follow-up activities with sentence strips and word cards. Whether the form of the language experience story is an individual story or the group chart story, it may be read again and again with the child's fluency skill improving with each reading. These stories may be collected and saved in a book to be read and reread as the child's skills develop. In addition, the stories may be duplicated and sent home to be read to parents.

Sound of the Letter Activity

In this component of the lesson, phonemic awareness is revisited. The sound of the targeted letter is reinforced with activities and games. The objective of these activities is to have the child listen for the sound. To accomplish this objective, pictures and objects of items depicting the featured sound need to be assembled. These pictures and objects are then used in games and activities in which the child listens to and recognizes the targeted sound.

Letter Identification Activity

The letter identification activity component of each lesson describes an activity in which the child learns to identify the targeted letter in a tactile and visual manner. It involves creating letters that use materials that are tangible and associated with the letter. For example, the children may be asked to glue lima beans onto the shape of the letter "L" on tag board pages (8½" × 11"). In this manner the child is provided a memorable way to identify and remember letters. These tag board pages are then secured together with a set of two or three large (three inch) key rings so that an alphabet book is constructed as each letter study activity is completed.

Play with Language

In this component of the lesson, you and the children are encouraged to be silly and playful with language. Nursery rhymes, chants, jokes, rhymes, jump rope rhymes, riddles, tongue twisters, and songs including rounds are employed in this section. While the children are having fun, they are acquiring more pieces of a basis of literacy: discriminating sounds, increasing the size of their oral vocabulary, improving their listening skills, and honing their ability to rhyme.

Poem

A poem citation or two are provided for each letter lesson. Within the context of *Teaching Phonemic Awareness through Children's Picture Books and Experiences,* the poems are included for enjoyment. They provide one more medium for hearing the sound of the letter. There's no call to launch into a heavy-handed lesson about symbolism, rhyme schemes, or arcane meanings. Read them so that the children may enjoy listening to poetry. I recommend that the poems be written on chart paper and placed on a chart rack so that they are accessible to the children to read again and again as their reading skills and strategies develop.

Supplementary Books

Additional titles are given at the end of each lesson. These books also include the targeted letter, are appropriate for reading aloud, and may lend themselves to experiential activities. It is suggested to have these books on hand and to use them to read aloud to bring the lesson into a full circle that goes from whole to part to whole. It may be that the teacher prefers to build a lesson around one of these books rather than the suggested lead book. For example, *The Runaway Rice Cake,* written by Ying Chang Compestine and illustrated by Tungwai Chau, makes an excellent lesson for "R."

Your Ideas

A section is provided at the end of each lesson for you. Here, add your own ideas for books, materials, and activities. As you read and carry out the lessons in this book, you may find yourself saying, "I know a better way to do this" or "I know just the book to read aloud for this letter" or "I know a sillier song." You are encouraged to be creative, to write down and use your own ideas.

THE ORGANIZATION OF THE BOOK

Teaching Phonemic Awareness through Children's Picture Books and Experiences consists of thirty lessons each consisting of nine components as described above. The contents are ordered alphabetically to facilitate searching for them. You may wish to consider a systematic order suggested by Gunning (2000): First, teach the lessons that introduce the letters in this set, but not necessarily in this order—S, M, B, F, R, hard G, L, hard C, N, H, T, D. Next, teach the lessons that introduce the letters in this set in order—J, P, W, K, Y, soft C, soft G, V, Z, Q. Finally, teach the lessons that emphasize the short vowel sounds and last, the long vowel sounds.

The lessons in this book are intended to be used with a group of children no larger than six who have a demonstrated assessed need for these lessons. I highly recommend that the lessons be set up as learning centers. Engage the assistance of paraprofessionals, parents, volunteers, and older children to help with the activities.

GETTING READY

Collect the picture books. Before beginning these lessons, gather the picture books and materials. Your public library is a great source for these books. If your local library does not have the books, order them through an interlibrary loan.

Construct a Phonemic Awareness Picture File. In addition, pictures and objects that match the letter sounds need to be gathered. Phonemic awareness activities require pictures and objects to elicit the targeted sound. To have these pictures on hand in an efficient manner, construct a Phonemic Awareness Picture File. Gathering and organizing pictures for the file can be a time-consuming task. What can be done to make this a fun activity?

1. Get help. Ask parents, friends, volunteers, teenage future teachers, retired people, paraprofessionals, and aides to help you find and prepare pictures.

2. Get organized. Obtain thirty file folders and have a storage container ready.

3. Gather materials. Have on hand scissors, construction paper, index cards, and glue. Ask your helpers to gather magazines, catalogs, coloring books, online clip art, clip art books, phonics workbooks, stickers, craft magazines, scrapbooking art, and scrapbooking books. Gunning's (2000) *Phonological Awareness and Primary Phonics* is an excellent source for pictures organized by letter sounds as is *Words Their Way* by Bear, Invernizzi, Templeton, and Johnston (2004). See Web sites and software titles that are sources for pictures and patterns in the resource section that follows.

4. Have a good time. Set aside a few hours for a cut and paste party. Invite your helpers. Play their favorite music and serve snacks while your helpers and you search the print materials for suitable items, cut out the pictures, and glue them onto construction paper and index cards. File alphabetically in the file folders so the pictures will be available when needed. Online clip art is a good source for phonemic awareness pictures.

Also, have on hand basic art and craft supplies such as glue, tag board, crayons, construction paper, clear tape, and scissors. Two three-inch key rings for the key ring alphabet book will be needed for each child. A few lessons require cooking ingredients, equipment, and utensils.

Once the books, materials, and equipment have been gathered and the players (the children and your helpers) have been assembled, you will be ready to create a literacy event as artful as a jazz piece, an opera, a symphony, or a master painting—lessons constructed to produce successful readers who are enchanted by books.

RESOURCES

Books

Songs and Rounds

Eddleman, David, ed. 1998. *The Great Children's Song Book.* Illustrated by Andrew J. Dowty. New York: Carl Fischer, Inc.

MacDonald, Margaret Read, & Winifred Jaeger. 1999. *The Round Book: Rounds Kids Love to Sing.* Illustrated by Yvonne LeBrun Davis. North Haven, CT: Linnet Books.

Silberg, Jackie, & Pam Schiller. 2002. *The Complete Book of Rhymes, Songs, Fingerplays, and Chants Poems.* Illustrated by Deborah C. Wright. Beltsville, MD: Gryphon House.

Poetry and Rhymes Anthologies

Cole, Johanna. 1989. *Anna Banana.* Illustrated by Alan Tiegreen. New York: Morrow Junior Books.

Harrison, Michael, & Christopher Stuart-Clark. 1988. *The Oxford Treasury of Children's Poems.* New York: Oxford University Press.

Hoberman, Mary Ann. *The Llama Who Had No Pajama.* Illustrated by Betty Fraser. San Diego: Harcourt Brace.

Prelutsky, Jack. 1983. *The Random House Poetry for Children.* Illustrated by Arnold Lobel. New York: Random House.

Sing a Song of Popcorn. 1988. Selected by Beatrice Schenk de Regniers, Eva Moore, Mary Michaels White, & Jan Carr. New York: Scholastic.

Activities to Do with Children Books

Bird, Malcolm, & Alan Dart. 1992. *The Magic Handbook.* San Francisco: Chronicle Books.

Blakey, Nancy. 1994. *More Mudpies 101 Alternatives to Television.* Berkeley, CA: Tricycle Press.

Blakey, Nancy. 1999. *The Mudpies Book of Boredom Busters.* Berkeley, CA: Tricycle Press.

Check, Laura. 2000. *Paper Plate Crafts.* Charlotte, VT: Williamson Publishing.

Jurenka, Nancy Allen. 2001. *Hobbies Through Children's Books and Activities.* Englewood, CO: Libraries Unlimited.

Kohl, Mary Ann F. 1985. *Scribble Cookies.* Bellingham, WA: Bright Ring Publishing.

Kohl, Mary Ann F. 1989. *Mudworks.* Illustrated by Kathleen Kerr. Bellingham, WA: Bright Ring Publishing.

Press, Judy. 1998. *Alphabet Art.* Illustrated by Sue Dennen. Charlotte, VT: Williamson Publishing.

Press, Judy. 2002. *All around the Town.* Charlotte, VT: Williamson Publishing.

Web Sites and Software

school.discovery.com/clipart/
webclipart.about.com
www.aaaclipart.com
www.abcteach.com

www.barrysclipart.com
www.clip-art.com
www.doverpublications.com
www.educplace.com
www.enchantedlearning.com
www.first-school.ws
www.janbrett.com
www.kidsdomain.com
www.nuttinbutkids.com
www.raffinews.com
www.songsforteaching.com
Kidspiration. Inspiration Software Inc. 7412 SW Beaverton Hillsdale Hwy, Suite 102. Portland, OR 97225-2167.

REFERENCES

Bear, Donald R., Marcia Invernizzi, Shane Templeton, & Francine Johnston. 2004. *Words Their Way,* 3rd ed. Upper Saddle River, NJ: Pearson Education.

Cunningham, James W., Patricia. M. Cunningham, James. V. Hoffman, & Hallie. K. Yopp. 1998. *Phonemic Awareness and the Teaching of Reading: A Position Statement from the Board of Directors of the International Reading Association.* Newark, DE: International Reading Association.

Fox, Barbara J. 2004. *Word Identification Strategies: Phonics from a New Perspective,* 3rd ed. Upper Saddle River, NJ: Pearson Prentice Hall.

Gunning, Thomas G. 2000. *Phonological Awareness and Primary Phonics.* Boston: Allyn & Bacon.

Hall, Mary Ann. 1978. *The Language Experience Approach for Teaching Reading: A Research Perspective.* Newark, DE: International Reading Association.

Lee, Dorris M., & Roach Van Allen.1963. *Learning to Read through Experience,* 2nd ed. New York: Appleton Century Crofts.

Reutzel, D. Ray, & Robert B. Cooter, Jr. 1996. *Teaching Children to Read,* 2nd ed. Upper Saddle River, NJ: Prentice Hall.

Reutzel, D. Ray, & Robert B. Cooter, Jr. 2004. *Teaching Children to Read,* 4th ed. Upper Saddle River, NJ: Pearson Education.

Snow, Catherine E., Susan M. Burns, & Peg Griffin. 1998. *Preventing Reading Difficulties in Young Children.* Washington, DC: National Academy Press.

Stauffer, Russell G. 1970. *The Language Experience Approach to the Teaching of Reading.* New York: Harper & Row.

Tompkins, Gail E. 2003. *Literacy for the 21st Century,* 3rd ed. Upper Saddle River, NJ: Prentice Hall.

Vacca, Jo Anne L., Richard T. Vacca, Mary T. Gove, Linda C. Burkey, Lisa A. Lenhart, & Christine A. McKeon. 2003. *Reading and Learning to Read,* 5th ed. Boston: Allyn & Bacon.

SHORT

A

Learning the Letter "A" (Short Sound)

Read Aloud

Spence, Rob, and Amy Spence. 1999. *Clickity Clack.* Illustrated by Margaret Spengler. New York: Viking Press.

Featured in this humorous rhyming tale about a train that accumulates more and more noisy creatures is a delightful collection of characters: talking yaks, seven tumbling acrobats, and a troupe of quacking ducks, to name a few. Finally, Driver Zach calls a halt to all the noise until the only sound is the wheels of the train going clickity clack. Spangler's lively illustrations add even more spark to the storyline. A delightfully perfect read aloud, you will find yourself being joined by the children as you repeatedly read this yarn to young readers. Have fun.

Read Aloud to Emphasize the Sound of Short "A"

Read a second time to emphasize the abundant number of short "A" words in the story. Rubber band the words so the children can easily hear the short "A" sounds such as: black, track, yaks, back, acrobats, quack, dancing, packs, Zach, attack, tack, sack, fact.

Experience-based Chart Story: Railroad Track Construction

MATERIALS: Chart paper, marker, tag board, twelve or more pieces of three-inch coffee stirrers, popsicle or craft sticks, glue, construction paper, pencils, clear tape, scissors, crayons, clean pint-sized milk cartons.

PROCEDURE: Have the children glue down the popsicle sticks on the tag board to create the train tracks cross pieces (ties). Have them roll strips of construction paper around their pencils to make tubes, secure the tubes with tape, and glue the paper tubes across the ties to create the tracks. Have them fashion a railroad car with wheels using the milk carton and construction paper. Put the children's railroad tracks on display.

After the train tracks have been constructed, gather the group in front of the chart paper and ask them to recount what occurred. On the chart paper write the group's recounting. Ask the children where they would like to go on their railroad tracks. Add your own sentences to include short

"A" words. In the days that follow, read and reread the chart story with your group. Hang it on a chart rack so it is available to the children for their reading enjoyment as their reading skills and strategies improve throughout the year.

As an alternative, distribute language experience paper. Have your group draw pictures about their train tracks and write scribble stories. Encourage them to include whatever letters they now know how to write. Have them dictate their scribble story to a "secretary"—you, an older student, a parent, or a volunteer.

Sound of the Letter Activity: Driver Zach's Train Game

MATERIALS: Train whistle, wagons for each child in the group, white roll paper, construction paper, tag board, tape.

PREPARATION: With the help of a volunteer, construct a paper railroad track around the room by drawing a track on white roll paper with a marker and laying the paper around the perimeter of the room. Write the consonants and consonant blends b, l, z, tr, cl, m, p, j, r, s, and t, along with key pictures for each, on separate pieces of tag board. Tape construction paper train-style wheels onto each wagon.

PROCEDURE: Teach the children this rhyme:

Clickity clack. Clickity clack.

-ack, -ack, -ack
Add the sound of ———(a consonant or consonant blend).

That makes
———ack, ———ack, ———ack.

Review the sounds of the consonants and blends in the game with the children.

Assign one child to be Driver Zach and give that child the train whistle. Give another child the stack of consonant cards. He or she will be the conductor. The remainder of the children pull the wagons around in a circle on the paper track forming the train. When Driver Zach blows the train whistle, the children pull their wagons around the track. When Driver Zach blows the train whistle the second time, the train stops and the children chant the rhyme. The child nearest the conductor inserts the sound of the consonant that the conductor holds up. Driver Zach blows the train whistle and the train starts up again. Repeat until all the consonants have been used.

Letter Identification Activity

MATERIALS: Tag board (8½" × 11", one for each child), glue, pipe cleaners, scissors.

PROCEDURE: Have the children write a large letter "A" on their tag boards. Have them glue the pipe cleaners in the form of railroad tracks to their letter. Tell the children to trace the letter with their fingers. Have them add this page to their key ring alphabet binder.

Play with Language

Have the children jump rope and chant the jump rope rhyme "Anna Banana." In *Anna Banana*, compiled by Joanna Cole. 1989. Illustrated by Alan Tiegreen. New York: Morrow Junior Books. p. 42.

Teach the children to sing "Little Red Caboose." In *The Complete Book of Rhymes, Songs, Poems, Fingerplays, and Chants,* compiled by Jackie Silberg & Pam Schiller. 2002. Illustrated by Deborah C. Wright. Beltsville, MD: Gryphon House. p. 248.

Poem

Jacobs, Frank. "The Bat." In *The Random House Poetry for Children,* selected by Prelutsky, Jack. 1983. Illustrated by Arnold Lobel. New York: Random House. p. 56.

Supplementary Books

Arnold, Marsha Diane. 2004. *Prancing, Dancing Lily.* Illustrated by John Manders. New York: Dial Books for Young Readers.

Banks, Kate. 2004. *The Cat Who Walked across France.* Illustrated by Georg Hallensleben. New York: Farrar, Straus and Giroux.

Helldorfer, M. C. 2004. *Got to Dance.* Illustrated by Hiroe Nikata. New York: Doubleday Books for Young Readers.

Hubbell, Will. 2002. *Apples Here.* Morton Grove, IL: Albert Whitman & Co.

Webb, Steve. 2003. *Tanka Tanka Skunk.* New York: Orchard Books.

Your Ideas

Use this space to record your own ideas for books, materials, and activities.

LONG

A

Learning the Letter "A" (Long Sound)

Read Aloud

Shannon, David. 2000. *The Rain Came Down.* New York: Blue Sky Press.

CB

The antics of the alarmed critters portrayed on the cover foretell this picture book's hilarity. Shannon is a master of illustrated facial expression. One episode after another is set off in domino order as each character reacts to a rain shower. Argument after argument is sparked until a hullabaloo ensues. The rain stops. The sun comes out. In reverse order the arguments turn into peaceful cooperation. Happiness reigns.

Read Aloud to Emphasize the Sound of Long "A"

Read aloud a second time. Rubber band the words so that the children can easily hear the long "A" sounds. The long "A" words are: came, made, rain, baby, away, plane, tomatoes, painter, paint, bakery, cakes, chasing, lady, rainbow, air, baker, bake, make, shave, A-OK, day.

Experience-based Chart Story: Rainy Days and Rainbows
Bulletin Board

MATERIALS: Chart paper, marker, gray and light blue construction paper, crayons, sentence strips, gray and blue butcher paper.

PREPARATION: Cover one half of a bulletin board with gray paper. Title this half "Rainy Days." Cover the other half with blue paper. Title this half "And Rainbows."

PROCEDURE: Day One: Engage the children in a brainstorming discussion about how they feel and what they do when the weather is gloomy, overcast, and rainy. Have them draw pictures of themselves on gloomy days on the gray paper. Have them dictate a caption to the picture to you. Write these on sentence strips.

Day Two: Engage the children in a brainstorming discussion about how they feel and what they do when a rainbow appears after a period of rain. Have them draw pictures of rainbow inspired activities and feelings on the light blue construction paper with crayons. Construct a bulletin board of their drawings and captions so as to contrast the rainy days and rainbow days.

After the bulletin board has been completed, gather the group in front of the chart paper and ask them to recount what occurred. On the chart paper write the group's recounting. Add your own sentences to include long "A" words. In the days that follow, read and reread the chart story with your group. Hang it on a chart rack so it is available to the children for their reading enjoyment as their reading skills and strategies improve throughout the year.

As an alternative, distribute language experience paper. After your group has drawn pictures about their rainy days and rainbows, have them write scribble stories. Encourage them to include whatever letters they now know how to write. Have them dictate their scribble story to a "secretary" (you, an older student, a parent, a volunteer).

Sound of the Letter Activity: Rainbow Mobiles

MATERIALS: Pictures from your Phonemic Awareness Picture File, coloring books, clip art, phonics workbooks, magazines, catalogs, glue, scissors, gray construction paper, manila drawing paper, crayons, yarn.

PROCEDURE: Have the children draw and cut out four raindrop shapes on the gray construction paper. Have the children search for pictures of items that contain the long "A" sound. Have them search the Phonemic Awareness Picture File, coloring books, catalogs, magazines, phonics workbooks, and clip art. Suggestions are: apron, cake, cage, snake, plate, tape, train, gate, face, ace, rain, lace, stage. Have them glue their pictures to construction paper raindrops. Have them draw a rainbow shape onto drawing paper and color the rainbow. Have them attach the raindrops to the rainbow with yarn. Hang their raindrop mobiles from the ceiling.

Letter Identification Activity

MATERIALS: Air dry modeling clay, tempera paint, tag board, glue.

PROCEDURE: With the modeling clay have the children construct an assortment of "A" letters, upper and lower case. When the clay has hardened, have the children paint their letters and glue their letters to tag board. Have the children trace the letters with their fingers. Tell them to place this page in their key ring alphabet binder.

Play with Language

Teach and sing the round "My Dame Has a Lame, Tame Crane." In *The Round Book: Rounds Kids Love to Sing,* by Margaret Read MacDonald & Winifred Jaeger. 1999. Illustrated by Yvonne LeBrun Davis. North Haven, CT: Linnet Books. p. 64.

Have the children chant the nursery rhyme "Patty Cake." Have the children chant the nursery rhyme "Rain Rain Go Away."

Poem

Schmeltz, Susan Alton. "Paper Dragons." In *The Random House Poetry for Children,* selected by Jack Prelutsky. 1983. Illustrated by Arnold Lobel. New York: Random House. p. 40.

Supplementary Books

Bunting, Eve. 2004. *My Special Day at Third Street School.* Illustrated by Suzanne Bloom. Honesdale, PA: Boyds Mill Press.

Compestine, Ying Chang. 2001. *The Runaway Rice Cake.* Illustrated by Tungwai Chau. New York: Simon & Schuster Books for Young Readers.

Donaldson, Julia. 2004. *The Snail and the Whale.* Illustrated by Axel Scheffler. New York: Dial Books for Young Readers.

Kurtz, Jane. *Rain Romp.* 2002. Illustrated by Dyanna Wolcott. New York: Greenwillow Books.

Provencher, Rose-Marie. 2004. *Slithery Jake.* Illustrated by Abby Carter. New York: HarperCollins.

Weatherford, Carole Boston. 2002. *Jazz Baby.* Illustrated by Laura Freeman. New York: Lee & Low.

Wells, Rosemary. 1997. *Bunny Cakes.* New York: Dial Books for Young Readers.

Your Ideas

Use this space to record your own ideas for books, materials, and activities.

B

Learning the Letter "B"

Read Aloud

Ryder, Joanne. 2002. *Big Bear Ball*. Illustrated by Steven Kellogg. New York: Harper-Collins.

⌈

Two prize-winning creators of children books got together to construct this romp. Steven Kellogg's exuberant illustrations turns Ryder's playful text into a party. Read aloud to enjoy the silliness and the happiness of the bears as they dance.

Read Aloud to Emphasize the Sound of the Letter "B"

Read aloud to emphasize the abundance of words that begin with "B." Have the children wave bear stick puppets when they hear the sound of "B" words in the story. These are: bushes, berries, bears, by, balloon, broad-beamed, big, ball, been, begin, beat.

Experience-based Chart Story: A Ball for Bears

MATERIALS: Chart paper, markers, paper plates, construction paper, crayons, scissors, glue, yarn or elastic band, bear mask pattern, audiotape/CD of "Turkey in the Straw" or other music appropriate for dancing the Virgina Reel, cloth or crepe paper sashes of two different colors.

PREPARATION: Help the children construct bear masks by attaching bear ears and a nose to paper plates. Mask examples may be found on Jan Brett's Web page (www.janbrett.com) and in *Paper Plate Crafts* by Laura Check.

PROCEDURE: Following these directions, teach the children to dance the Virginia Reel. Have a ball.

Virginia Reel Directions

Reel Step One. Arrange the children into two parallel lines identified by the color of their sashes (Color A, Color B).

Reel Step Two. Have all the children in both lines step forward and back in eight beats. That would be four steps forward and four steps back to place.

Reel Step Three. Have all the children in both lines extend their right hands to their partners (the person across from them). Tell them to turn their partners by walking around their partners while holding hands and going back in place in line in eight beats.

Reel Step Four. Have the children in both lines extend their left hands to their partners. Tell them to turn their partners and go back in place in line in eight beats.

Reel Step Five. Have the partners do-si-do and return to place in eight beats. Do-si-do is a square dance movement in which the partners move toward each other, pass, and cross back to back before returning to place.

Reel Step Six. Have the top couple meet in the middle, join both hands, slide step down the line between the dancers, and slide step back to place.

Reel Step Seven. Have the top couple hook right elbows and turn one and a half turns so that each partner is facing the next child in the opposite line. Color A partner swings the next child in the Color B line by hooking elbows and Color B partner swings the next child in the Color A line. Have the top couple come back to the middle of the formation, hook elbows, turn, and repeat the process until all the children in both lines have been turned. This is the reel step from which the dance gets its name. Have the top couple meets at the bottom of the formation and slide step back to the top.

Reel Step Eight. Have the top couple separate and turn to the outside of the line and walk to the end. All the other children follow them.

Reel Step Nine. Have the top couple meet at the bottom of the formation and form an arch. The other couples dance under the arch. The top couple stays at the bottom. The new top couple repeats the dance. The dance is repeated until all couples have had a turn being the top couple.

After the ball, gather the group in front of the chart paper. Ask them to dictate to you what occurred during their Ball for Bears. On the chart paper write the group's recounting. Add your own sentences to include "B" words. In the days that follow, read and reread the chart story with your group. Hang it on a chart rack so it is available to the children for their reading enjoyment as their reading skills and strategies improve throughout the year.

As an alternative, distribute language experience paper. Have your group draw pictures about the Ball for Bears and write scribble stories. Encourage them to include whatever letters they now know how to write. Have them dictate their scribble story to a "secretary" (you, an older student, a parent, a volunteer).

Sound of the Letter Activity: Favors for the Ball

MATERIALS: Clear tape, small objects that begin with the letter "B"—for example, barrettes, tiny balls, beads, mini sizes of candy bars such as Butterfingers, bubble gum, jelly beans, butterscotch—and lengths of crepe paper streamers about thirty-six inches in length, one for each child in the group.

PREPARATION: Tape the small items onto the crepe paper. Roll the crepe paper into a ball and secure with stickers of items that begin with "B."

PROCEDURE: This is a fun activity. Reassure the children that they get to keep the items in each ball. Distribute the "B" balls to each child before they go home from school on the day of the Ball for Bears. Draw their attention to the stickers. Listen as they point to the stickers and identify the "B" words.

Letter Identification Activity

MATERIALS: Crushed butterscotch candy, tag board, glue.

PROCEDURE: Have the children write a large letter "B" on the tag board. Have them glue the crushed butterscotch candy to the letter's outline. After the glue has dried, have the children trace the letter with their fingers. Tell the children to place this page in their key ring alphabet binder. *Suggestion:* Distribute one candy to each child to eat while doing this activity.

Play with Language

Have the children create riddles, the answers to which begin with "B." For example, "It's what you do when you make a cake." Answer: "bake." Good words to suggest are: bat, butter, ball, brake, bee, bounce, banana, bird. Have the children sing the songs "Bingo" or "Bibbidi-Bobbidi-Boo."

Alternative: Obtain and teach your class to sing and do the actions for *Bernie Bear* available from: Penny and Pals. Kids Kollectibles. Playground Publishing. 1104 Second Avenue S., Suite 313. Fargo, ND 58103. (701) 293-8004; (800) 895-KIDS. www.pennyandpals.com.

Poem

Hoberman, Mary Ann. 1998. "Rabbit." In *The Llama Who Had No Pajama.* Illustrated by Betty Fraser. San Diego: Harcourt Brace. p. 18.

Supplementary Books

Accorsi, William. 1992. *Billy's Button.* New York: Greenwillow Books.

Corey, Shana. 2002. *Ballerina Bear.* Illustrated by Pamela Paparone. New York: Random House.

Henkes, Kevin. 1995. *The Biggest Boy.* Illustrated by Nancy Tafuri. New York: Greenwillow Books.

Kelley, True. 2001. *Blabber Mouse.* New York: Dutton Children's Books.

Massie, Diane Redfield. 1963 (Text) and 2000 (Illustrations). *The Baby Beebee Bird.* Illustrated by Steven Kellogg. New York: HarperCollins.

Nolen, Jerdine. 1994. *Harvey Potter's Balloon Farm.* Illustrated by Mark Buehner. New York: Mulberry Books.

Sierra, Judy. 1999. *Tasty Baby Belly Buttons.* Illustrated by Meilo So. New York: Dragonfly Books.

Stadler, Alexander. 2003. *Beverly Billingsly Takes a Bow.* San Diego: Harcourt Brace.

Wheeler, Lisa. 2004. *Bubble Gum, Bubble Gum.* Illustrated by Laura Huliska-Beith. New York: Little, Brown.

Your Ideas

Use this space to record your own ideas for books, materials, and activities.

SOFT

C

Learning the Letter "C" (Soft Sound)

Read Aloud

Jackson, Ellen. 1994. *Cinder Edna*. Illustrated by Kevin O'Malley. New York: Lothrop, Lee & Shepard Books.

In this reincarnation of the old tale, we meet a down to earth young woman, Cinder Edna. She is Cinderella's upbeat neighbor. When the night of the ball occurs, Cinder Edna wears her loafers and takes the bus. Cinder Edna dances the night away with the prince's brother with whom she has a lot in common—an interest in recycling, telling jokes, and tuna casseroles. At the stroke of midnight, both Cinderella and Cinder Edna bolt for the door leaving their footwear behind. Eventually, both princes find their respective girls. Cinderella lives in the castle and is bored beyond measure while Edna and her prince tell jokes, laugh, and take in stray kittens. O'Malley's zany illustrations match the wacky tone of this retold old tale.

Read Again to Emphasize the Sound of Soft "C"

Read aloud a second time to emphasize the soft "C" words. These are: cinders, cinnamon, ceremony, ceremonies, cement, cinder, Cinderella, Cinder Edna, recycled.

Experience-based Chart Story: Recycling Party

In *Cinder Edna* the importance of being self-reliant and having a positive attitude are emphasized. Prepare to have a Cinder Edna Recycling Party. Have the children clean up trash to recycle. In the spirit of Cinder Edna, have them learn jokes to tell at the party. Have the children gather newspapers and aluminum cans to be taken to the recycling center. Have a party.

MATERIALS: Chart paper, markers, food for a party including cider, jokes, scrip (play money or tokens), scale, wagons.

PREPARATION: Arrange with fellow teachers to have their classes save aluminum cans and/or newspaper for two weeks. Decide how much scrip needs to be prepared to compensate the children for the aluminum cans and newspapers that they will collect. Arrange with volunteers to take the items to a recycling center.

PROCEDURE: Have your group go from classroom to classroom collecting the aluminum cans and newspaper each day. For every pound of paper and every aluminum can, put scrip into a glass jar so everyone can see how much scrip is being raised. When the amount of scrip reaches X point (decide this ahead of time), have a volunteer take the recycled items to your nearest recycling center. Have a party. Ask the children to share jokes. Serve refreshments.

After the group has gathered in front of the chart paper, ask them to recount their experiences with recycling and the party. On the chart paper write the group's recounting. Add your own sentences to include soft "C" words.

As an alternative, distribute language experience paper. Have your group draw pictures about the recycling activity and party and write scribble stories. Encourage them to include whatever letters they now know how to write. Have them dictate their scribble story to a "secretary" (you, an older student, a parent, a volunteer).

Sound of the Letter Activity: Soft "C" Treasure Hunt

MATERIALS: Pictures of items that start with soft "C" from the Phonemic Awareness Picture File, workbooks, coloring books, clip art, catalogs, magazines. When "C" is followed by the letter "e" as in "cent," "i" as in "city," or "y" as in "cycle," it has a soft sound. Words to use for this lesson include: cedar, cement, cellular phone, cellophane, center, certain, cereal, cider, cinder, Cinderella, cinchy, circus, circle, city, cyclist, cymbals. Index cards or tag board, glue, cinnamon cereal, pictures of items that do not start with soft "C."

PREPARATION: Glue pictures to the cards. Hide the cards around the room.

PROCEDURE: Divide the children into pairs or triads. Have them search for picture cards of items that begin with the soft "C" sound. Award each pair with pieces of cinnamon cereal for each correct picture that they find.

Letter Identification Activity

MATERIALS: Cinnamon cereal, glue, tag board.

PROCEDURE: Ask the children to write a large letter "C" on their tag board. Have the children glue cinnamon cereal to the letter "C." Have the children trace the letter with their fingers. Tell them to place this page in their key ring alphabet binder.

Play with Language

Have the children learn and sing "The Cinderella Work Song" from the Disney video. It can be accessed at www.stlyrics.com/lyrics/cinderella/theworksong.htm.

Poem

Prelutsky, Jack. "City, Oh, City!" In *The Random House Poetry for Children,* selected by Jack Prelutsky. 1983. Illustrated by Arnold Lobel. New York: Random House. p. 89.

Supplementary Books

Engel, Diana. 1999. *Circle Song.* New York: Marshall Cavendish.

Henkes, Kevin. 1998. *Circle Dogs.* Illustrated by Dan Yaccarino. New York: Greenwillow Books.

Rice, Eve. 1987. *City Night.* Illustrated by Peter Sis. New York: Greenwillow Books.

Rosten, Norman. 2004. *A City Is.* Illustrated by Melanie Hope Greenberg. New York: Henry Holt.

Sanderson, Ruth. 2002. *Cinderella.* New York: Little, Brown.

Tiller, Ruth. 1993. *Cinnamon, Mint & Mothballs.* Illustrated by Aki Sogabe. San Diego: Browndeer Press.

Your Ideas

Use this space to record your own ideas for books, materials, and activities.

HARD
C

Learning the Letter "C" (Hard Sound)

Read Aloud

Stevens, Janet, & Susan Stevens Crummel. 1999. *Cook-a-Doodle-Doo!* Illustrated by Janet Stevens. San Diego: Harcourt Brace.

CB

Big Brown Rooster has had it with chicken feed. He wants something delicious like his Great-Granny Little Red Hen made. A search of the hen house results in finding her cookbook and, like his ancestor, his requests for help from the barnyard animals are rebuffed. He is about to launch into making strawberry shortcake all by himself but Iguana, Turtle, and Potbellied Pig show up with offers to help. Chaos ensues, but all turns out well in the end. This uproarious reworking of the old story combined with Janet Stevens' comic drawings guarantee a happy time in the classroom.

Read Aloud to Emphasize the Sound of Hard "C"

Read a second time, putting emphasis on words that begin with the hard "C" sound. Have the children wave rooster stick puppets (rooster sticker or rubber stamped figure glued to a craft stick) when they hear the hard "C" sound and chant, "cock a doodle doo." Words in the story that begin with hard "C" are: can, coop, cookbook, cook, cat, cooked, cooking, cups, carefully, cup, counting, cut, cool, caught.

Experience-based Chart Story: Cooking Experience—Making Strawberry Shortcake

MATERIALS: Flour, sugar, baking powder, salt, butter, one egg, milk, strawberries, whipping cream. Mixing bowls, whisk, spoons, baking pans, bowls for serving, spoons, oven. The recipe for making Great-Granny's Magnificent Strawberry Shortcake is found at the end of *Cook-A-Doodle-Doo!*

PREPARATION: Divide the tasks, ingredients, and utensils among the children.

PROCEDURE: Help the children follow the recipe to make the shortcake. Eat and enjoy.

After the cooking experience, gather the group in front of the chart paper. Ask them to recount what occurred. On the chart paper write the group's recounting. Add your own sentences to include hard "C" words. In the days that follow, read and reread the chart story with your group. Hang it on a chart rack so it is available to the children for their reading enjoyment as their reading skills and strategies improve throughout the year.

As an alternative, distribute language experience paper. Have your group draw pictures about the cooking experiences and write scribble stories. Encourage them to include whatever letters they now know how to write. Have them dictate their scribble story to a "secretary" (you, an older student, a parent, a volunteer).

Sound of the Letter Activity: Sorting

MATERIALS: Index cards, glue, pictures from your Phonemic Awareness Picture File and other sources of pictures such as catalogs, magazines, phonics workbooks, clip art, and Web sites. Create sets of ten pictures of items that begin with hard "C" such as can, cat, cake, comb, coat, cub, card, cup, corn, and car. Also create a set of ten pictures of items that do not begin with "C" for each child in your group.

PROCEDURE: Have the children sort their cards by placing the "C" sounds in one row and the non-"C" sounds in another row.

Letter Identification Activity

MATERIALS: Electric warming tray, crayons, 8½" × 11" paper, glue, tag board.

PROCEDURE: Have the children write the letter "C" repeatedly with crayons on paper that has been placed on the warming tray turned on low heat. Glue the paper to the tag board to be placed in their key ring alphabet binders. Ask the children to trace the letter "C" with their fingers.

Play with Language

Sing the round "The Cuckoo." In *The Round Book: Rounds Kids Love to Sing,* by Margaret Read MacDonald & Winifred Jaeger. 1999. Illustrated by Yvonne LeBrun Davis. North Haven, CT: Linnet Books. p. 39.

Poems

Carryl, Charles Edward. "The Song of the Camel." In *The Oxford Treasury of Children's Poems,* compiled by Michael Harrison & Christopher Stuart-Clark. 1988. New York: Oxford University Press. p. 118.

Hoberman, Mary Ann. 1998. "Cookie Magic." In *The Llama Who Had No Pajama.* Illustrated by Betty Fraser. San Diego: Harcourt Brace. p. 32.

Supplementary Books

Baker, Keith. 1997. *Cat Tricks.* San Diego: Harcourt Brace.

Banks, Kate. 2004. *The Cat Who Walked across France.* Illustrated by Georg Hallensleben. New York: Farrar, Straus & Giroux.

Oller, Erika. 2004. *The Cabbage Soup Solution.* New York: Dutton Children's Books.
O'Malley, Kevin.1999. *Leo Cockroach . . . Toy Tester.* New York: Walker & Co.
Rylant, Cynthia. 1999. *The Cookie-Store Cat.* New York: Blue Sky Press.
Stevens, Janet. 1993. *Coyote Steals the Blanket.* New York: Holiday House.

Your Ideas

Use this space to record your own ideas for books, materials, and activities.

D

Learning the Letter "D"

Read Aloud

Shannon, David. 2002. *Duck on a Bike.* New York: Blue Sky Press.

ᚙ

All the barnyard animals have opinions about Duck riding a bicycle around the barnyard but they keep their thoughts to themselves. Nevertheless, it is obvious from their expressions that they would all love to ride a bike, so when a group of children show up and park their bikes outside the farmhouse, the animals take advantage of this opportunity. They each grab a bike and begin riding gleefully about. Shannon's illustrations portray the animals' emotions with great clarity. The expressions range from disdain, disgust, jealousy, envy, and hopeful desire, to delirious happiness. Read aloud to enjoy Shannon's humor.

Read Aloud to Emphasize the Sound of "D"

Read a second time. Have the children wave duck stick puppets every time the "D" sound is heard. The word "duck" is repeated on nearly every page.

Experience-based Chart Story: Observing a Duck and Writing a Poem

MATERIALS: Chart paper, marker, domesticated live duck, cage, duck food, water, newspaper.
PREPARATION: Arrange to have a live domesticated duck brought to your classroom in a large cage provisioned with food and water. Set the cage on thick layers of newspaper or appropriate materials for easy clean up.
PROCEDURE: Have the children observe the appearance and behavior of the duck. Have them draw pictures of the duck.

Construct a chart poem with a repeated line. Follow this pattern and write it on the chart paper:

Line one: Our duck is a dandy, downy duck.

Line Two: Our duck is _____(adjective)

Line Three: Our duck _____(verb phrase)

Line Four: Our duck _____(verb phrase)

Line Five: Our duck is a dandy, downy duck.

Have the children compose the poem with you. Place the poem in a spot where the children will be able to read their poem repeatedly over the weeks to follow.

As an alternative, have on hand an assortment of stuffed toy ducks.

Sound of the Letter Activity: Duck Shape Books

MATERIALS: Pattern of duck (see www.abcteach.com) for the book's front and back covers and the inside pages, construction paper, lined paper, the Phonemic Awareness Picture File and other sources of pictures such as catalogs, phonics workbooks, magazines, coloring books, clip art.

PREPARATION: Using the duck pattern, cut front and back covers from construction paper and the inside pages from lined writing paper. Staple together. Make enough books for each member of the group.

PROCEDURE: Have the children search for, cut out, and glue pictures of items starting with "D" into their duck books. Suggestions of items to look for include: daffodil, daisy, dalmatian, deer, desk, dirt, dish, dog, doll, dress, drum, duck.

Letter Identification Activity

MATERIALS: Tag board, white glue, brayer, liquid tempera paint, liquid detergent, cookie sheet with a lip.

PREPARATION: Add a few drops of liquid detergent to the tempera paint when ready to print. It helps the paint flow more easily.

PROCEDURE: Have the children write large letters "D," lower and upper case on the tag board. Have them outline their letters with white glue. After the glue has hardened (may take overnight), have the children roll the brayer in the paint and then over the letters. Have them place a paper over the painted raised letters and rub the paper with their hands to obtain a print of the letters. When the paint has dried have the child place this page in their key ring alphabet binder.

Play with Language

Teach and sing the round "Oh How Lovely Is the Evening." In *The Round Book: Rounds Kids Love to Sing,* by Margaret Read MacDonald & Winifred Jaeger. 1999. North Haven, CT: Linnet Books. p. 33.

Have them play the playground game Duck Duck Goose.

Poem

Lewis, Emily. "My Dog." In *The Oxford Treasury of Children's Poem,* compiled by Michael Harrison & Christopher Stuart-Clark. 1988. New York: Oxford University Press. p. 89.

Supplementary Books

Alborough, Jez. 2001. *Fix-It Duck*. New York: HarperCollins.

Alborough, Jez. 2003. *Captain Duck*. New York: HarperCollins.

Buzzeo, Toni. 2003. *Dawdle Duckling*. Illustrated by Margaret Spengler. New York: Dial Books for Young Readers.

Cronin, Doreen. 2002. *Giggle, Giggle, Quack*. Illustrated by Betsy Lewin. New York: Simon & Schuster Books Young Readers.

Cronin, Doreen. 2004. *Duck for President*. Illustrated by Betsy Lewin. New York: Simon & Schuster Books for Young Readers.

Jenkins, Emily. 2004. *Daffodil*. Illustrated by Tomek Bogacki. New York: Farrar, Straus & Giroux.

Shannon, George. 1982. *Dance Away*. Illustrated by Jose Aruego & Ariane Dewey. New York: Greenwillow Books.

Thompsen, Lauren. 2003. *Little Quack*. Illustrated by Derek Anderson. New York: Simon & Schuster Books for Young Readers.

Whybrow, Ian. 2004. *Harry and the Dinosaur Say "Raahh!"*. Illustrated by Adrian Reynolds. New York: Random House.

Your Ideas

Use this space to record your own ideas for books, materials, and activities.

SHORT

E

Learning the Letter "E" (Short Sound)

Read Aloud

Galdone, Paul. 1998. *The Little Red Hen.* Boston: Clarion Books.

The little red hen wishes to make a cake but the dog, the cat, and the mouse all refuse to help her with the work. They are, however, eager to benefit from her labors. They learn their lesson and soon start to help around the house.

Read Aloud to Emphasize the Letter "E" (Short Sound)

Read aloud a second time. Words that have a short "E" sound in the Galdone story are: red, hen, beds, swept, mended, when, then, eggs, them, whenever. Emphasize the sound of short "E" by using the rubber banding technique described in the Introduction.

Experience-based Chart Story: Bread Pretzels

MATERIALS: Chart paper, markers. For each child, have on hand a strip of unlined paper, 3"×48" adding machine tape folded back and forth so as to have a series of three-inch squares. For the pretzels, have on hand yeast, flour, sugar, salt, water, shortening, one egg white, and sea salt as well as bowls, spoon for stirring, baking sheet, and towels. A recipe for pretzels is at the end of this lesson.

PROCEDURE: Be sure children wash their hands before starting this activity. Assign a task to everyone. Make the dough. Knead. Have the children roll out and form the dough into pretzels. Allow to rise. Bake half of the dough for eating. Save the other half for making letters for their key ring alphabet binders (see Letter Identification Activity).

After the children have gathered around a table, distribute the folded paper strips to each child. Discuss how the bread pretzel dough was made. Have them draw a picture in each square to show the sequence in which the dough was made and the pretzels were shaped and baked.

After the bread pretzel making sequence stories have been drawn, gather the group in front of the chart paper, ask them to recount what occurred. On the chart paper write the group's recounting. Add your own sentences to include short "E" words. In the days that follow, read and reread the chart story with your group. Hang it on a chart rack so it is available to the children for their reading enjoyment as their reading skills and strategies improve throughout the year.

Sound of the Letter Activity: Egg Basket Bulletin Board

MATERIALS: Construction paper, glue, tag board, egg patterns, pictures of items of short "E" words from your Phonemic Awareness Picture File and other sources of pictures such as coloring books, phonics workbooks, magazines, catalogs, clip art, and Web sites.

PREPARATION: Cover a bulletin board with white paper and draw a simple farm scene. Draw a very large red hen and the outline of a basket.

PROCEDURE: Have the children search the Phonemic Awareness Picture File as well as coloring books, phonics workbooks, magazines, catalogs, clip art, and Web sites for pictures of items that contain the short "E" sound. These may include: hen, vet, sled, letter, jet, pets, red, bread, pretzel, den, bed, net, egg, vest. Have the children glue their short "E" pictures to their eggs. Tell the children to attach the construction paper eggs to the basket.

Letter Identification Activity

MATERIALS: The other half of the pretzel dough, tag board, glue, Mod Podge, brush.

PROCEDURE: Have the children form the pretzel dough into two letter "E"s, upper and lower case. Have the children bake and eat one of them. Have them glue the other "E" to their tag board pages, brush the bread pretzel "E" with Mod Podge, and insert the page into their key ring alphabet binder.

Play with Language

Have the children learn and tell egg jokes. For example, "What do you call an egg that crossed the Sahara Desert?" Answer: "An egg-splorer." More egg jokes may be found on the Internet at www.goldenegg.com.

Poem

Hoberman, Mary Ann. 1998. "Meg's Egg." In *The Llama Who Had No Pajama*. Illustrated by Betty Fraser. San Diego: Harcourt Brace. p. 37.

Supplementary Books

Asch, Frank. 1998. *Ziggy Piggy and the Three Little Pigs*. Tonawanda, NY: Kids Can Press.

Auch, Mary Jane. 1996. *Eggs Mark the Spot*. New York: Holiday House.

Barton, Byron. 1993. *The Little Red Hen*. New York: HarperCollins.

Bridwell, Norman. 1998. *Clifford, the Big Red Dog*. New York: Scholastic.

Cronin, Doreen. 2004. *Duck for President*. Illustrated by Betsy Lewin. New York: Simon & Schuster Books for Young Readers.

Heine, Helme. 1983. *The Most Wonderful Egg in the World.* New York: Atheneum Books for Young Readers.

Hull, Rod. 2000. *Mr. Betts and Mr. Potts.* Illustrated by Jo Davies. Cambridge, MA: Barefoot Books.

Peek, Merle.1985. *Mary Wore Her Red Dress and Henry Wore His Green Sneakers.* Boston: Clarion Books.

Bread Pretzel Recipe

1 package of yeast	1½ cups of warm water
1 teaspoon salt	1 tablespoon sugar
4 cups flour	egg white

Dissolve the yeast in warm water. Stir in the sugar. Let the mixture stand for a few minutes. Add the salt and flour. Mix. Turn out onto a floured board. Knead. Place back into the bowl. Cover with a cloth. Allow dough to rise until double in size. Divide the dough among the children. Have them form the dough into pretzels. Place on baking sheet. Brush with egg white. Sprinkle on salt. Bake for fifteen minutes at 350 degrees.

Your Ideas

Use this space to record your own ideas for books, materials, and activities.

LONG

E

Learning the Letter "E" (Long Sound)

Read Aloud

Udry, Janice May. 1956. *A Tree Is Nice*. Illustrated by Marc Simont. New York: Harper & Row.

ॐ

In this Caldecott Medal winner, Udry tells a heartwarming story in which the reader comes to know the various seasons and uses for a tree. Marc Simont's prizewinning illustrations are as attractive today as they were in 1956.

Read Aloud to Emphasize the Sound of Long "E"

Read aloud to emphasize the long "E" sound. Rubber band the sound to make it more easily heard. Have the children wave tree-shaped stick puppets (a tree shape glued to a craft stick) whenever they hear the sound of long "E." Words that include long "E" are: trees, beside, valleys, even, tree, because, leaves, breeze, see, lean, near, keeps, years.

Experience-based Chart Story: Plant a Tree

MATERIALS: Chart paper, marker, tree seedling, digging tools, water, a spot that receives at least six hours of sun each day.

PREPARATION: Have the spot chosen and the tools and tree seedling ready to go. Review the directions for planting a tree seedling with your group of children. If you are not sure about how to plant a tree, check out the Web site www.kidsface.org/pages/plant.html.

PROCEDURE: Have the children take turns digging the hole. Have one of them free the tree seedling from its container. Have the children plant the tree and refill the hole with soil. Be sure it is well watered at planting time and in the weeks that follow.

After the tree is planted, gather the group in front of the chart paper. Ask them to recount what occurred. Write the group's recounting. Add your own contribution to be sure long "E" words are included.

Sound of the Letter Activity: Tree Bulletin Board

MATERIALS: Construction paper, brown kraft paper, leaf patterns, scissors, glue. Also have a bulletin board covered with blue and green paper to represent the sky and grass. Have on hand long "E" pictures from the Phonemic Awareness Picture File as well pictures from other sources such as coloring books, magazines, phonics workbooks, clip art, and Web sites.

PREPARATION: Have sufficient leaf patterns on tag board for each child in your group. Construct a tree by twisting the brown kraft paper and stapling it to the bulletin board so as to have a trunk and several branches. Set out long "E" pictures from your Phonemic Awareness Picture File.

PROCEDURE: Have the children find pictures of items that have long "E" sounds. Suggestions are: tree, leaves, cream, street, bean, seat, meat, beets, sheep, queen, wheel, green, feet, beach. Have them glue their pictures to construction paper leaves. Attach the leaves to the tree.

Letter Identification Activity

MATERIALS: Cheese dough (recipe at the end of the lesson). White bread (one slice for each child), white glue, water, small bowls for each child.

PROCEDURE: Be sure children wash their hands before starting this activity. Have the children roll the dough into coils. Have them form the coils into the letter "E." Bake, eat, and enjoy these cheesy "E"s. For the letter "E" to be placed in the alphabet binder, mix up a batch of bread dough clay. Again, be sure children have washed their hands. Have each child mix together one slice of white bread (crust removed), one tablespoon of white glue, and $1/4$ teaspoon water. Tell the children to knead the dough until it no longer sticks to their fingers. Have the children roll the dough into ropes and form the letter "E." This clay will dry overnight. The next day tell the children to paint the letter "E" with clear nail polish or Mod Podge and glue the letters to tag board. Have them add this page to their key ring alphabet binder.

Play with Language

Teach and sing the round "To Ope Their Trunks." In *The Round Book: Rounds Kids Love to Sing,* by Margaret Read MacDonald & Winifred Jaeger. 1999. Illustrated by Yvonne LeBrun Davis. North Haven, CT: Linnet Books. p. 13.

Poem

Silverstein, Shel. "Tree House." In *Sing a Song of Popcorn,* selected by Beatrice Schenk de Regniers, Eva Moore, Mary Michaels White, & Jan Carr. 1988. New York: Scholastic. p. 99.

Supplementary Books

Cox, Judy. 2004. *Go To Sleep, Groundhog!* Illustrated by Paul Meisel. New York: Holiday House.

Fox, Mem. 2004. *Where Is the Green Sheep?* Illustrated by Judy Horacek. San Diego: Harcourt Brace.

Ginsburg, Mirra. 1992. *Asleep. Asleep.* Illustrated by Nancy Tafuri. New York: Greenwillow Books.

Manushkin, Fran. 1994. *Peeping and Sleeping.* Illustrated by Jennifer Plecas. Boston: Clarion Books.

Polacco, Patricia. 1993. *The Bee Tree.* New York: Philomel Books.

Ryder, Joanne. 1991. *Hello Tree!* Illustrated by Michael Hays. New York: Dutton Lodestar Books.

Shaw, Nancy E. 1999. *Sheep in a Jeep.* Boston: Houghton Mifflin.

Cheesy "E" Dough Recipe

1 cup of flour	1 cup of shredded cheese
$\frac{1}{3}$ cup shortening	3 tablespoons water

Mix the ingredients. Divide dough into handful size hunks. Roll the dough into coils. Form into letters. Place on greased cookie sheet. Bake for five minutes at 400 degrees.

Your Ideas

Use this space to record your own ideas for books, materials, and activities.

F

Learning the Letter "F"

Read Aloud

Pfister, Marcus. 2002. *The Rainbow Fish*. New York: North-South Books.

Rainbow Fish learns that it is better to share and have friends than to be handsome and lonely. Once he begins to share his beautiful scales with the other fish, he gains companionship. This story about the most beautiful fish in the world has spawned a continuing series of Rainbow Fish books.

Read Aloud to Emphasize the Sound of "F"

Read aloud a second time to emphasize the sound of F. Have the children wave fish stick puppet (a fish shape glued to a craft stick) whenever they hear the sound of "F." Words to emphasize when the story is read a second time are: followed, friends, from, fin, friend, fish, flashing, filled, felt, finally, feeling.

Experience-based Chart Story: Goldfish Care

MATERIALS: Chart paper, marker, goldfish, fishbowl, marbles, dechlorinated water (tap water that has stood for twenty four hours to eliminate the chlorine), fish food, fish net.

PREPARATION: Place the marbles in the bottom of the fishbowl. Fill the bowl with dechlorinated water. Add the goldfish.

PROCEDURE: Have children care for the goldfish following directions provided by you. Be sure the water is changed daily and that new dechlorinated water is ready to be used. Have the children wash the bowl, being sure to rinse out all the soap. Do not overfeed the fish. Follow the directions on the food packet. The life of the fish depends on following these directions.

After the group has gathered in front of the chart paper, create a chart recounting the directions for fish care. Add your own sentences to include "F" words. In the days that follow, read and reread the chart story with your group. This would also be an opportune time for your children to share the directions with another class that has a fish so they can follow them and your children can witness the value of written communication. Again, have them emphasize the importance of following directions to the life of the fish.

As an alternative, distribute language experience paper. Have your group draw pictures about the goldfish care and write scribble stories. Encourage them to include whatever letters they now know how to write. Have them dictate their scribble story to a "secretary" (you, an older student, a parent, a volunteer).

Sound of the Letter Activity: Fishing Game

MATERIALS: Fish pattern, paper clips, construction paper, small magnets, string, dowel, glue, a bucket. Pictures of items that do and do not begin with the letter "F" from your Phonemic Awareness Picture File and other sources such as magazines, catalogs, coloring books, phonics workbooks, clip art, and Web sites. Suggestions are: face, family, fan, fawn, feather, fence, fish, foot, football, fox, fin.

PREPARATION: Construct a fish game by gluing pictures to construction paper fish shapes and attaching a paper clip to each fish. Construct a fishing pole by attaching a magnet to one end of a string and tying the string to a dowel. Put the paper fish in a container such as a bucket.

PROCEDURE: Have each child in turn dip the fishing pole into the bucket and catch a fish. The child may keep the fish if it has an item beginning with the sound of "F."

Letter Identification Activity

MATERIALS: Tag board, glue, fuzzy fabric scraps.

PROCEDURE: Have the children write a large letter "F" on their tag board. Have them glue fuzzy fabric scraps to the letter. Tell the children to trace the letter with their fingers. Have them put this page in their key ring alphabet binder.

Play with Language

Have the children sing "The Farmer in the Dell."

Poem

Farjeon, Eleanor. "Bedtime." In *The Oxford Treasury of Children's Poems,* compiled by Michael Harrison & Christopher Stuart-Clark. 1988. New York: Oxford University Press. p. 149.

Supplementary Books

Alborough, Jez. 2001. *Fix-It Duck.* New York: HarperCollins.

Cates, Karin. 2002. *A Far-Fetched Story.* Illustrated by Nancy Carpenter. New York: Greenwillow Books.

Edwards, Pamela Duncan. 1995. *Four Famished Foxes and Fosdyke.* Illustrated by Henry Cole. New York: HarperCollins.

Flora, James. 1994. *The Fabulous Firework Family.* New York: Margaret K. McElderry Books.

Fox, Mem. 1992. *Hattie and the Fox.* Illustrated by Patricia Mullins. New York: Aladdin.

Galdone, Paul. 1971. *Three Aesop Fox Fables.* New York: Seabury Press.

Your Ideas

Use this space to record your own ideas for books, materials, and activities.

SOFT
G

Learning the Letter "G" (Soft Sound)

Read Aloud

Galdone, Paul. 2002. *The Gingerbread Boy.* Boston: Houghton Mifflin.

CB

In this version of the old story the reader is treated to Paul Galdone's style of writing that lends itself so well to being read aloud. His humorous paintings match the story's tone. The fox is as wily and self-satisfied as ever after swallowing that clever cookie that escapes his pursuers. This version of the story is available in a tape/book combination.

Read Aloud to Emphasize the Sound of Soft "G"

Read the story, emphasizing the words that have the soft "G" sound. Have the children wave gingerbread boy stick puppets whenever they hear a soft "G" sound. In this book these words are the repetition of "gingerbread." Use a gingerbread cookie cutter for the pattern for the stick puppet. Glue construction paper shape to a craft stick.

Experience-based Chart Story: Gingerbread Boy Cookies

MATERIALS: Chart paper, marker, gingerbread cookie dough, gingerbread boy cookie cutter, purchased cake decorating frosting in tubes.

PROCEDURE: If possible, make the gingerbread cookies from scratch together with the children. Otherwise, have the baked, undecorated cookies available to be decorated by the children.

Have students wash their hands. Distribute the cookies and the tubes of frosting and have the children decorate their gingerbread boys.

After the group has gathered in front of the chart paper, ask them to recount the sequence of what occurred. Add your own sentences to assure that soft "G" words are included in the recounting, for example: generous, ginger, germs, gee-whiz, gingerbread.

As an alternative, distribute language experience paper. Have your group draw pictures about the cookie baking experience and write scribble stories. Encourage them to include whatever letters they now know how to write. Have them dictate their scribble story to a "secretary" (you, an older student, a parent, a volunteer).

Sound of the Letter Activity: Giant Gingerbread Boy

MATERIALS: Two lengths of brown kraft paper, each at least eight feet long, newspaper for stuffing, yarn or twine for hanging. Pictures of "G" words from your Phonemic Awareness Picture File as well as pictures from sources such as catalogs, coloring books, clip art, phonics workbooks, magazines, Web sites, and children's drawings. Soft "G" words include: gentle, giant, ginger, gingerbread, gem, germs, gym, gentleman, geography, geology, geometry, general (a military title), gel, gelato, gelatin, gesture, giraffe.

PREPARATION: Draw two eight-foot giant gingerbread boys on the brown kraft paper. Cut out these two figures. These will be the front and back of one giant gingerbread boy. As a suggestion, ask an adult to be the model for the outline for the gingerbread boy.

PROCEDURE: Have children glue the front and back pieces together around the edges, leaving an opening. Have them stuff him with newspaper. Decorate as desired. Cover his front and back with soft "G" pictures. Attach the yarn to the top of his head and the shoulders. Hang the stuffed gingerbread boy from the ceiling.

Letter Identification Activity

MATERIALS: Gingerbread cookie crumbs, glue, tag board, pencils.

PROCEDURE: Tell the children to write a large letter "G" in upper and lower case on tag board. Have the children glue cookie crumbs to the outline of the letters on the tag board. Have them add this page to their key ring alphabet binder.

Play with Language

Using the soft "G" words given above, have the children construct silly sentences in which most of the words begin with soft "G." Have them illustrate their sentences.

Poem

Silverstein, Shel. 1964. *A Giraffe and a Half*. New York: HarperCollins.

Supplementary Books

Aggs, Patrice. 1999. *The Visitor*. New York: Orchard Books.

Andreae, Giles. 1999. *Giraffes Can't Dance*. Illustrated by Guy Parker-Rees. New York: Orchard Books.

Ernst, Lisa Campbell. 1990. *Ginger Jumps*. New York: Bradbury Press.

Loredo, Elizabeth. 2004. *Giant Steps*. Illustrated by Barry Root. New York: G. P. Putnam's Sons.

Rey, H. A. 1998. *Curious George*. Boston: Houghton Mifflin.

Your Ideas

Use this space to record your own ideas for books, materials, and activities.

HARD
G

Learning the Letter "G" (Hard Sound)

Read Aloud

Finch, Mary. 2001. *Three Billy Goats Gruff.* Illustrated by Roberta Arenson. Cambridge, MA: Barefoot Books.

This version of the traditional tale is written in a way that makes reading aloud a joy. Finch's version includes a purple-clawed singing troll. Arenson's colorful collages create a book with a happy look. Her pink, yellow, and blue goats prance around a sunny landscape. Finch has written the text so that it lends itself to role-playing.

Read Aloud to Emphasize the Sound of Hard "G"

Read aloud a second time to emphasize the sound of hard "G." Have the children wave a goat stick puppet whenever they hear the sound of hard "G." These are: goat, green, grass, grow, greener, getting.

Experience-based Chart Story: Play Acting

This story lends itself to theater—storytelling, retelling as a flannel board story, puppet show, readers theatre, a simple play. For the purposes of this lesson, a role-playing activity is suggested.

MATERIALS: Paper plates, construction paper, glue, elastic bands.

PREPARATION: Construct goat and troll masks from paper plates. Use your own imagination or go to www.janbrett.com or *Paper Plate Crafts* by Laura Check for ideas. Assign the parts. Distribute the masks.

PROCEDURE: Appoint a reader (an older child, parent, volunteer, yourself). Have the children pantomime their parts while the story is read. Put on the play for another class.

After the play has been given, have the children recount their experiences putting on the play.

As an alternative, distribute language experience paper. Have your group draw pictures about the play and write scribble stories. Encourage them to include whatever letters they now know how to write. Have them dictate their scribble story to a "secretary" (you, an older student, a parent, a volunteer).

Sound of the Letter Activity: Gee Whiz/Good Golly Tic Tac Toe

MATERIALS: Tic tac toe game boards/papers, game pieces—tiny gingerbread men and goat figures (these could be stickers or rubber stamp figures) glued to corks, bottle caps, or erasers.

PROCEDURE: Pair up the children. Each child in a pair thinks of "G" word appropriate for his or her game piece. The child playing with the goat game pieces thinks of words with a hard "G" sound. The child playing with the soft "G" sound thinks of words that have a soft "G" sound. The children in turn pronounce their words and place a game piece on a square. The game continues until three spaces in a row up, down, or diagonally are filled. The soft "G" player declares victory by saying "Gee whiz." The hard "G" player declares victory by saying "Good Golly."

Letter Identification Activity

MATERIALS: Gumdrops, glue, tag board.

PROCEDURE: Have the children glue gumdrops to their tag boards on which they have written upper and lower case "G." Have them trace the letter "G" with their fingers. Tell the children to place this page in their key ring alphabet binders.

Play with Language

Teach and sing the round "Why Shouldn't My Goose." In *The Round Book: Rounds Kids Love to Sing,* by Margaret Read MacDonald & Winifred Jaeger. 1999. Illustrated by Yvonne LeBrun Davis. p. 63. North Haven, CT: Linnet Books.

Poems

Dugan, Michael. "Gumble." In *The Random House Poetry for Children,* selected by Jack Prelutsky. 1983. Illustrated by Arnold Lobel. New York: Random House. p. 209.

Hoberman, Mary Ann. 1998. "Good Morning When It's Morning." *The Llama Who Had No Pajama.* Illustrated by Betty Fraser. San Diego: Harcourt Brace.

Supplementary Books

Alakija, Polly. 2002. *Catch That Goat.* Cambridge, MA: Barefoot Books.

Castle, Caroline. 2000. *Gorgeous!* Illustrated by Sam Childs. New York: Crown.

Cronin, Doreen. 2002. *Giggle, Giggle, Quack.* Illustrated by Betsy Lewin. New York: Simon & Schuster Books for Young Readers.

Dunrea, Oliver. 2002. *Gossie.* Boston: Houghton Mifflin.

Gugler, Laurel Dee, & Clare Beaton. 2003. *There's a Billy Goat in the Garden.* Illustrated by Clare Beaton. Cambridge, MA: Barefoot Books.

Kadair, Deborah Ousley. 2003. *Grandma's Gumbo.* Gretna, LA: Pelican Publishing Company.

Offen, Hilda. 1995. *Good Girl, Gracie Growler.* Milwaukee, WI: Gareth Stevens Publishing.

Polacco, Patricia. 2004. *Oh, Look!* New York: Philomel Books.
Shannon, Margaret. 1998. *Gullible's Troubles.* Boston: Houghton Mifflin.

Your Ideas

Use this space to record your own ideas for books, materials, and activities.

H

Learning the Letter "H"

Read Aloud

Ashman, Linda. 2001. *Castles, Caves, and Honeycombs.* Illustrated by Lauren Stringer. San Diego: Harcourt Brace.

ଔ

Various animals and objects are associated with their homes in Linda Ashman's charming rhyming text. Warm illustrations create the cozy feelings of a series of homes.

Read Aloud to Emphasize the Sound of "H"

Read a second time to emphasize these words: home, heap, honeycomb, hole, hollow, home's, house, hug.

Experience-based Chart Story: Constructing Houses

MATERIALS: Chart paper, marker, shoeboxes, construction paper, scissors, glue. Pictures from your Phonemic Awareness Picture File as well as pictures from other sources such as catalogs, clip art, magazines, coloring books, phonics workbooks, and Web sites.

PROCEDURE: Have the children construct and decorate houses out of shoeboxes and construction paper. Have the children find, cut out, and paste pictures of "H" items onto construction paper. Suggestions are: hollyhock, house, hummingbird, hoe, hockey, honey, hook, hammer, hand, hen, hug. These are stored in their "H" houses. Display. After the group has gathered in front of the chart paper, ask them to recount what items they have in their houses. This recounting will be in a list form. For example:

Jim has a horse, ham, and a hat in his house.

Megan has a hat, a hippo, and a hose in her house.

And so on.

Sound of the Letter Activity: Sound Houses

Using the shoebox houses that the children constructed, have them share the pictures of items that begin with "H."

Letter Identification Activity

Mix up a batch of half a cup of liquid starch and one cup of dry tempera paint. Divide by pouring portions onto paper plates. Distribute among the children. Tell the children to press the palms of their hands in the mixture and to form the letter "H" on a piece of tag board by making several prints of their hand with their fingers held together (not spread). After the "H" handprints have dried, have the children place this page of handprint "H"s in their key ring alphabet binders.

Play with Language

Teach and have the children sing the round "Sweetly Sings the Donkey." In *The Round Book: Rounds Kids Love to Sing,* by Margaret Read MacDonald & Winifred Jaeger. 1999. Illustrated by Yvonne LeBrun Davis. North Haven, CT: Linnet Books. p. 52.

Have the children learn and recite the nursery rhyme "Humpty Dumpty."

Poems

Guiterman, Arthur. "The Habits of the Hippopotamus." In *The Random House Poetry for Children,* selected by Jack Prelutsky. 1983. Illustrated by Arnold Lobel. New York: Random House. p. 191.

Reeves, James. "Animal Houses." In *The Oxford Treasury of Children's Poems,* compiled by Michael Harrison & Christopher Stuart-Clark. 1988. New York: Oxford University Press. p. 87.

Supplementary Books

Alborough, Jez. 2002. *Hug.* New York: Cambridge Press.

Bramhall, William. 2004. *Hepcat: Live in Concert.* New York: Philomel Books.

Brett, Jan. 2000. *Hedgie's Surprise.* New York: G. P. Putnam's Sons.

Diakite, Baba Wague. 1999. *The Hatseller and the Monkeys.* New York: Scholastic.

Galdone, Paul. 1998. *The Little Red Hen.* Boston: Houghton Mifflin.

Hoberman, Mary Ann. 1978. *A House Is a House for Me.* Illustrated by Betty Fraser. New York: Viking Press.

Martin, Bill. 1991. *The Happy Hippopotami.* Illustrated by Betsy Everitt. San Diego: Harcourt Brace.

Van Camp, Richard. 1998. *What's the Most Beautiful Thing You Know about Horses?* Illustrated by George Littlechild. San Francisco: Children's Book Press.

Your Ideas

Use this space to record your own ideas for books, materials, and activities.

SHORT

I

Learning the Letter "I" (Short Sound)

Read Aloud

Shannon, George. 2003. *Tippy-Toe Chick, Go!* Illustrated by Laura Dronzek. New York: Greenwillow Books.

ଔ

In simple text and repeated lines, George Shannon tells the story of triumph that all youngest family members will appreciate. Laura Dronzek's bright green backgrounds combined with reds and yellows set a summer lawn scene in which Clever Little Chick outsmarts Dog. She maneuvers Dog to wrap himself around a tree trunk. When Dog is safely secured, Little Chick leads her family to the garden.

Read Aloud to Emphasize the Sound of Short "I"

Read aloud a second time. Rubber band the words so the children can easily hear the "I" sounds. The short "I" words in this story include: tippy-toe, chick, little, chicks, itty-bitty, with, this, into, promised, big, listen, his, wing, middle, it, without, yip, think.

Experience-based Chart Story: Caring for Baby Chicks

MATERIALS: Chart paper, marker, baby chicks, cage, chick food, water, newspaper, heat lamp.

PREPARATION: Arrange to have baby chicks brought to your classroom in a large cage provisioned with food and water. Be certain that the heat lamp is set at the appropriate height and temperature; otherwise, the chicks' health will be compromised. Set the cage on thick layers of newspaper or appropriate materials for easy clean up.

PROCEDURE: Have the children observe the appearance and behavior of the baby chicks. Have them draw pictures of the baby chicks.

After the group has gathered in front of the chart paper, ask them to recount what occurred. On the chart paper write the group's recounting. Add your own sentences to include short "I" words. In the days that follow, read and reread the chart story with your group. Hang it on a chart rack so it is available to the children for their reading enjoyment as their reading skills and strategies improve throughout the year.

As an alternative, distribute language experience paper. Have your group draw pictures about the chicks and their care. Have the children write scribble stories. Encourage them to include whatever letters they now know how to write. Have them dictate their scribble story to a "secretary" (you, an older student, a parent, a volunteer).

Sound of the Letter Activity: Tippy Toe Chick Tic Tac Toe

MATERIALS: Five small pictures of words that include short sound of "I," such as clip, skip, lid, chick, bin, chip, dip, kid, pit, pin, stick thin, pig, wig, kick, lip. In addition, have small pictures of dogs (stickers work well), ten index cards, glue.

PREPARATION: Glue dog pictures to five of the index cards and pictures of items that have short "I" to other five index cards. Prepare a tic tac toe game board by drawing the grid on a large sheet of construction paper or poster board. Review how to play tic tac toe with the children.

PROCEDURE: Have pairs of children play Tippy Toe Chick Tic Tac Toe with the index cards with short "I" sounds (these represent the chicks) on one side of the tic tac toe game board and dog index cards on the other.

Letter Identification Activity

MATERIALS: Tag board, glue, tiny sticks.

PROCEDURE: Have the children write a large letter "I" on the tag board. Have them glue the tiny sticks to the outline. Tell them to trace the stick letter "I" with their fingers. Have them place these tag board pages in their key ring alphabet binders.

Play with Language

Have your children jump rope to the "Miss" jump rope rhyme. In *Anna Banana,* compiled by Joanna Cole. 1989. Illustrated by Alan Tiegreen. p. 43. New York: Morrow Junior Books.

Poems

Hoberman, Mary Ann. 1998. "Rabbit." *The Llama Who Had No Pajama.* Illustrated by Betty Fraser. San Diego: Harcourt Brace. p. 18.

Ipcar, Dahlov. "Fishes' Evening Song." In *The Random House Book of Poetry,* selected by Jack Prelutsky. 1983. Illustrated by Arnold Lobel. New York: Random House. p. 78.

Supplementary Books

Bell, Babs. 2004. *The Bridge Is Up!* Illustrated Rob Hefferan. New York: HarperCollins.

Brett, Jan. 1989. *The Mitten.* New York: G. P. Putnam's Sons.

Galdone, Paul. 1998. *The Three Little Pigs.* Boston: Houghton Mifflin.

Harper, Charise Mericle. 2004. *Itsy Bitsy, the Smart Spider.* New York: Dial Books for Young Readers.

Leuck, Laura. 2003. *One Witch.* Illustrated by S. D. Schnindler. New York: Walker & Co.

Long, Melinda. 2001. *Hiccup Snickup.* Illustrated by Thor Wickstrom. New York: Simon & Schuster Books for Young Readers.

Root, Phyllis. 2000. *Kiss the Cow.* Illustrated by Will Hillenbrand. Cambridge, MA: Candlewick Press.

Your Ideas

Use this space to record your own ideas for books, materials, and activities.

LONG
I

Learning the Letter "I" (Long Sound)

Read Aloud

Sendak, Maurice. 1992. *Chicken Soup with Rice.* Music by Carole King. Norwalk, CT: Weston Woods.

CB

This edition of Sendak's book of months is packaged as a book/audiotape combination that features the music of Carole King. In poetic form Sendak enumerates and describes a boy's love of chicken soup with rice every month of the year.

Read Aloud to Emphasize the Sound of Long "I"

Read aloud a second time. Rubber band the words so the children can easily hear the long "I" sounds. Words with a long "I" sound in this story include: ice, nice, sliding, twice, rice, lightly, inside, while, Nile, ride, crocodile.

Experience-based Chart Story: Ice Cube Candles

MATERIALS: Chart paper, marker, four-inch candles or candle stubs, modeling clay, clean pint-sized milk cartons, ice cubes, paraffin, hot plate, old double boiler, gallon Ziploc bags, mallet or rolling pins.

PREPARATION: Melt the paraffin in the top of the double boiler. Be careful to keep the children at a safe distance. Distribute milk cartons, modeling clay, candle stub, ice, and Ziploc bags to the children.

PROCEDURE: While the paraffin is melting, have the children anchor their candle stubs with modeling clay inside the milk cartons. Then have the children crush the ice cubes by pounding them in the plastic bags with a mallet. Next, tell them to fill the milk cartons with crushed ice. Have an adult fill each of the cartons with the melted paraffin. After the paraffin has hardened, have the children take the milk carton to the sink to peel off the carton and let the water from the melted ice cubes run out. The design of each candle will differ because of the holes created by the melted ice cubes. Encourage conversation about the children's ice cube candles.

After the ice cube candle making experience, gather the group in front of the chart paper and ask them to recount what occurred. Lead them to discuss why the candles have holes. On the chart paper write the group's recounting. Add your own sentences to include "I" words. In the days that follow, read and reread the chart story with your group. Hang it on a chart rack so it is available to the children for their reading enjoyment as their reading skills and strategies improve throughout the year.

As an alternative, distribute language experience paper. Have your group draw pictures about the ice cube candle making experience and write scribble stories. Encourage them to include whatever letters they now know how to write. Have them dictate their scribble story to a "secretary" (you, an older student, a parent, a volunteer).

Sound of the Letter Activity: Long "I" Rhyme Game

MATERIALS: A dime, toy mice, and a light bulb. Nine pieces of colored construction paper squares for each child, one color for each child. A list of words, some of which rhyme with "dime," "mice," or "light" and some of which do not. Appropriate rhyming words are: lime, time, crime, nice, dice, rice, bright, fight, sight. Add your own nonrhyming words.

PREPARATION: Place the dime, the toy mice, and the light bulb on a table in front of the children. Distribute the construction paper squares so that each child has a different color.

PROCEDURE: Instruct the children to listen for a word that rhymes with one of the three items as you pronounce the words on your list. Tell them that when they hear a rhyming word, they should place one of their paper squares under the item with which the word rhymes.

Letter Identification Activity

MATERIALS: Tag board, glue, uncooked rice.

PROCEDURE: Have the children write a large letter "I" on their tag board. Have them glue rice to the letter outline. Tell the children to trace the "I" letter with their fingers. Have them place this page in their key ring alphabet binder.

Play with Language

Have the children sing "Three Blind Mice."

Poems

Fyleman, Rose. "Mice Are Nice." In *Sing a Song of Popcorn,* selected by Beatrice Schenk de Regniers, Eva Moore, Mary Michaels White, & Jan Carr. 1988. New York: Scholastic. p. 71.

Hoberman, Mary Ann. 1998. "Ice-Skating." In *The Llama Who Had No Pajama.* Illustrated by Betty Fraser. San Diego: Harcourt Brace. p. 25.

Supplementary Books

Ashman, Linda. 2004. *Just Another Morning.* Illustrated by Claudio Munoz. New York: HarperCollins.

Compestine, Ying Chang. 2001. *The Runaway Rice Cake.* Illustrated by Tungwai Chau. New York: Simon & Schuster Books for Young Readers.

Harper, Charise Mericle. 2004. *Itsy Bitsy, the Smart Spider.* New York: Dial Books for Young Readers.

Hayes, Geoffrey. 2004. *Night-Light for Bunny.* New York: HarperCollins.

Hoff, Syd. 1988. *Mrs. Brice's Mice.* New York: Harper & Row.

Pinkwater, Daniel. 2001. *Cone King: The Scary Ice Cream Giant.* Illustrated by Jill Pinkwater. New York: Scholastic.

Yaccarino, Dan. 2001. *The Lima Bean Monster.* Illustrated by Adam McCauley. New York: Walker & Co.

Your Ideas

Use this space to record your own ideas for books, materials, and activities.

J

Learning the Letter "J"

Read Aloud

Weatherford, Carole Boston. 2002. *Jazz Baby*. Illustrated by Laura Freeman. New York: Lee & Low Books.

⛃

This infectious chant will get children on their feet and dancing. So be prepared for snapping fingers and wiggling bodies as you read Weatherford's happy text. Be sure to share with your group the expressive illustrations that enliven the poem.

Read Aloud to Emphasize the Sound of "J"

Read aloud the book for a second time. Before you read it, tell your group to raise their hands above their bodies and sway every time you come to a word that begins with the "J" sound. Read the chant emphasizing the "J" sound and the word "Jazz." Have fun.

Experience-based Chart Story: Jazzy Conga Line

MATERIALS: Rhythm instruments, chart paper, marker.
PROCEDURE: Get your group on their feet and form a conga line. Hand out the rhythm instruments. Have an experienced reader (a fifth grader, a parent volunteer, a paraprofessional, or a high school or university student) read the chant a third time as a child leads the conga line around the classroom. Play the instruments. Wiggle. Jump. Clap. Stomp. Twirl. Have fun.

After the group has gathered in front of the chart paper, ask them to recount what happened. On the chart paper write the group's recounting. Add your own sentences to include "J" words. In the days that follow, read and reread the chart story with your group. Hang it on a chart rack so it is available to the children for their reading enjoyment as their reading skills and strategies improve throughout the year.

As an alternative, distribute language experience paper. Have the children draw pictures and write scribble stories about their Jazzy Conga Line experience. Encourage them to include whatever letters they now know how to write. Ask each child to dictate his or her story to you while you write the story under the scribble writing.

Sound of the Letter Activity: Going to Jamaica

MATERIALS: A list of questions and answers:

We're going to Jamaica.	
How will we get there?	Jet, jeep
When will we go?	January, June, July
What will we wear?	Jeans, jodhpurs, jackets
What will we drink?	Jugs of juice
What will we eat?	Jars of jellybeans, jam, and jelly
What will we play?	Jacks, jump rope
What will we win?	Jackpot
What will we hear?	Jazz, jokes
What will we dance?	Jitterbug
How will we feel?	Jolly

PROCEDURE: Start the activity by announcing, "We are going to Jamaica," followed by the first question. Wait for a response from the children. The first time around, allow them to come up with their own responses and accept any that make sense and begin with "J." Add your own. Go to the next question and repeat the process. Play the game several times, refining it each time. It may become rhythmic. Just see what happens.

Letter Identification Activity

MATERIALS: Tag board, glue, jimmies, Mod Podge.
PROCEDURE: Have the children write the letter "J" on the tag board, glue jimmies to the "J" shape, and coat the letter with Mod Podge. Allow the letter to dry. Have them trace over the letter "J" with their fingers. Tell them to place this page in their key ring alphabet binder.

Play with Language

Have the children learn and sing the campfire song "John Jacob Jingleheimer Schmidt." In *The Complete Book of Rhymes, Songs, Poems, Fingerplays, and Chants,* compiled by Jackie Silberg & Pam Schiller. 2002. Illustrated by Deborah C. Wright. Beltsville, MD: Gryphon House. p. 227.

Teach and sing "Jenny Jones." In *The Great Children's Song Book,* edited by David Eddleman. 1998. Illustrated by Andrew J. Dowty. New York: Carl Fischer, Inc. p. 20.

Poem

Milne, A. A. "Disobedience." In *The Oxford Treasury of Children's Poems,* compiled by Michael Harrison & Christopher Stuart-Clark. 1988. New York: Oxford University Press. pp. 62–63.

Supplementary Books

Christelow, Eileen. 1989. *Five Little Monkeys Jumping on the Bed.* Boston: Clarion Books.

Henkes, Kevin. 1989. *Jessica.* New York: Greenwillow Books.

Hicks, Ray, & Lynn Salsi. 2000. *The Jack Tales.* Illustrated by Owen Smith. CD included. New York: Callaway.

Ogburn, Jacqueline K. 1998. *The Jukebox Man.* Illustrated by James Ransome. New York: Dial Books for Young Readers.

Stevens, Janet. 2003. *Jackalope.* Illustrated by Susan Stevens Crummel. San Diego: Harcourt Brace.

Van Laan, Nancy. 1998. *So Say the Little Monkeys.* Illustrated by Yumi Heo. New York: Atheneum Books for Young Readers.

Your Ideas

Use this space to record your own ideas for books, materials, and activities.

K

Learning the Letter "K"

Read Aloud

McKee, David. 2000. *Elmer and the Kangaroo.* New York: HarperCollins.

႗ჽ

Elmer, the patchwork elephant, along with Lion and Tiger, meets Kangaroo, who is upset because he can't jump. Kangaroo is worried that he won't perform well in an upcoming jumping contest. Elmer notices that Kangaroo bounces quite well. He encourages Kangaroo to think of jumping as bouncing, a mental trick that works. Using it, Kangaroo wins the contest.

Read Aloud to Emphasize the Sound of "K"

Read aloud to focus on words that start with "K." Words that start with the letter "K" in this book are repetitions of "kangaroo."

Experience-based Chart Story: Kangaroo Kiss Cookies and Kool-Aid

MATERIALS: Chart paper, marker, sugar cookie dough, rolling pins, cookie sheets, waxed paper, flour, Hershey's Kisses, kangaroo-shaped cookie cutters.

PROCEDURE: Have the children wash their hands before working with the sugar cookie dough. Divide the cookie dough among the children. Have them roll out their pieces of dough to $1/8$" thickness on floured waxed paper. Have them take turns sharing the kangaroo-shaped cookie cutter. Bake the cookies in a 375-degree oven for four minutes. Remove the cookie sheet and place an unwrapped Hershey Kiss on each cookie. Finish baking for three more minutes and let cool. Serve with Kool-Aid. Eat and enjoy.

After the cookies are baked, gather the group in front of the chart paper and ask them to recount what occurred. On the chart paper write the group's recounting. Add your own sentences to include "K" words. Suggestion: "Kids get a kick out of making cookies." In the days that follow, read and reread the chart story with your group. Hang it on a chart rack so it is available to the children for their reading enjoyment as their reading skills and strategies improve throughout the year.

As an alternative, distribute language experience paper. Have your group draw pictures about baking Kangaroo Kiss Cookies and write scribble stories. Encourage them to include whatever letters they now know how to write. Have them dictate their scribble story to a "secretary" (you, an older student, a parent, a volunteer).

Sound of the Letter Activity: Kangaroo Bulletin Board

MATERIALS: Construction paper and glue. Pictures of items that begin with "K" from the Phonemic Awareness Picture File and other sources such as magazines, clip art, catalogs, picture Web sites, and phonics workbooks. Suggestions are: kernels, kite, kiss, kettle, kit, kitten, king, key, keg, kangaroo.
PREPARATION: Construct a bulletin board on which a very large kangaroo is drawn. Have on hand tag board kangaroo patterns for tracing.
PROCEDURE: Have the children trace a kangaroo on construction paper. Have the children glue pictures of items that start with "K" to their kangaroos. Attach the construction paper kangaroos to the large kangaroo on the bulletin board.

Letter Identification Activity

MATERIALS: Kernels of corn, tag board, glue.
PROCEDURE: Have the children write a large letter "K" on their tag board and glue the kernels to it. Have them put this page in their key ring alphabet binders.

Play with Language

Teach and sing the round "Kookaburra." In *The Round Book: Rounds Kids Love to Sing,* compiled by Margaret Read MacDonald & Winifred Jaeger. 1999. Illustrated by Yvonne LeBrun Davis. North Haven, CT: Linnet Books. p. 74. It may also be found in *The Complete Book of Rhymes, Songs, Poems, Fingerplays, and Chants,* compiled by Jackie Silberg & Pam Schiller. Illustrated by Deborah C. Wright. Beltsville, MD: Gryphon House. p. 231.

Teach and sing "K-K-K-Katy." Lyrics can be accessed at www.rienzihills.com.

Poem

Moore, Margaret, & John Travers. "K." In *Sing a Song of Popcorn,* selected by Beatrice
     Schenk de Regniers, Eva Moore, Mary Michaels White, & Jan Carr. 1988. New
     York: Scholastic. p. 5.

Supplementary Books

Burton, Virginia Lee. 1971. *Katy and the Big Snow.* Boston: Houghton Mifflin.
Galdone, Paul. 1999. *Three Little Kittens.* Boston: Houghton Mifflin.
Henkes, Kevin. 2004. *Kitten's First Full Moon.* New York: Greenwillow Books.

Payne, Emmy. 1944. *Katy No-Pocket*. Illustrated by H. A. Rey. Boston: Houghton Mifflin.

Penn, Audrey. 1993. *The Kissing Hand*. Illustrated by Ruth E. Harper & Nancy M. Leak. Washington, DC: The Child Welfare League of America.

Rey, Margaret.1958. *Curious George Flies a Kite*. Illustrated by H. A. Rey. Boston: Houghton Mifflin.

Root, Phyllis. 2000. *Kiss the Cow*. Illustrated by Will Hillenbrand. Cambridge, MA: Candlewick Press.

Spalding, Andrea. 2003. *The Most Beautiful Kite in the World*. Illustrated by Leslie Watts. Toronto: Fitzhenry & Whiteside.

Your Ideas

Use this space to record your own ideas for books, materials, and activities.

L

Learning the Letter "L"

Read Aloud

Yaccarino, Dan. 2001. *The Lima Bean Monster.* Illustrated by Adam McCauley. New York: Walker & Co.

Sammy hates lima beans. He discovers a way to rid himself of them so Mom does not catch on. He buries them in a hole in the yard after hiding them in his socks to get them out of the house. The neighborhood kids discover that they can bury in that hole everything that they dislike, from distasteful veggies to failing spelling papers. Unfortunately, a huge storm causes a ferocious vegetable monster to emerge from the hole. This monster has a taste for human beings and begins grabbing up the grown-ups. Sammy saves the day by having his friends eat their vegetables by chomping away at the monster.

Read Aloud to Emphasize the Sound of "L"

Read the story a second time, emphasizing the sound of "L." Words that begin with "L" in this story are: life, long, live, last, let, long, like, listened, lightning, little, lots, looked, laughed, luck.

Experienced-based Chart Story: Lima Bean Monsters

MATERIALS: Chart paper and marker. Dried lima beans painted with green tempera paint, glue, construction paper, black crayons, writing paper.
PROCEDURE: Have the children draw an outline of a monster with black crayon. Have them glue the green painted beans within the outline.

Have each of them write scribble stories about their monster. Have them dictate their scribble story to a "secretary" (you, an older student, a parent, a volunteer). Make a bulletin board display of their stories and artwork.

After the monster creation and story writing activities, gather the group in front of the chart paper and ask them to recount what occurred. On the chart paper write the group's recounting. Add your own sentences to include "L" words. In the days that follow read and reread the chart story with your group. Hang it on a chart rack so it is available to the children for their reading enjoyment as their reading skills and strategies improve throughout the year.

Sound of the Letter Activity: "L" Concentration

MATERIALS: Pictures of items beginning with "L" such as lace, lion, lollipop, lamb, licorice, lamp, lily, light bulb, log. Have a set of pictures of items that do not begin with "L," index cards, glue. Pictures may be obtained from the Phonemic Awareness Picture File and other sources of pictures such as magazines, coloring books, clip art, catalogs, picture Web sites, and phonics workbooks.

PREPARATION: Glue the pictures to index cards.

PROCEDURE: Place the cards face down on a tabletop. Have children, in turn, turn the cards over two at a time to pair pictures of items that begin with "L." The players who find a pair of items that begin with "L" may keep the pair and score a point.

Letter Identification Activity

MATERIALS: Dry lima beans, glue, tag board.

PROCEDURE: Have the children construct the letter "L" with dry lima beans. Tell them to trace the lima bean letter with their fingers. Have the children add this page to their key ring alphabet binder.

Play with Language

Have the children draw pictures of tongue twisters. For example, a child might draw and share a picture that illustrates "Lovable Lulu liked to lick licorice laces." Have them think of a sentence with all or most of the words beginning with "L." Have them illustrate their sentences and then orally share what the tongue twister is.

Poem

Hoberman, Mary Ann. 1998. "Foxes." In *The Llama Who Had No Pajama*. Illustrated by Betty Fraser. San Diego: Harcourt Brace. p. 27.

Supplementary Books

Bogan, Paulette. 2003. *Goodnight Lulu.* London: Bloomsbury Children's Books.

Bozylinsky, Hannah Heritage. 1993. *Lala Salama: An African Lullaby in Swahili and English.* New York: Philomel Books.

Dunbar, Joyce. 1991. *Lollopy.* Illustrated by Susan Varley. New York: Macmillan.

Edwards, Pamela Duncan. 2004. *The Leprechaun's Gold.* Illustrated by Henry Cole. New York: HarperCollins.

Laguna, Sofie. 2004. *Too Loud Lily.* Illustrated by Kerry Argent. New York: Scholastic.

O'Malley, Kevin. 1999. *Leo Cockroach . . . Toy Tester.* New York: Walker & Co.

Stanley, Mandy. 2004. *Lettice the Flying Rabbit.* New York: Simon & Schuster Books for Young Readers.

Waber, Bernard. 1969. *Lovable Lyle.* Boston: Houghton Mifflin.

Your Ideas

Use this space to record your own ideas for books, materials, and activities.

M

Learning the Letter "M"

Read Aloud

Ashman, Linda. 2001. *Maxwell's Magic Mix-Up*. Illustrated by Regan Dunnick. New York: Simon & Schuster Books for Young Readers.

In this zany story, an inept party magician turns the birthday girl into a rock and party goers into a bird, a cat, and a pig. Father is transformed into a broom. Chaos grows but the magician's nephew, Alex, saves all. Dunnick's cartoon-like illustrations add to the delightful wackiness of Ashman's poem. A well-rehearsed read-aloud will fill your classroom with hoots and hollers.

Read Aloud to Emphasize the Sound of "M"

Read aloud a second time. Have the children wave magic wands when they hear the sound of "M." Magic wands may be constructed of aluminum foil wrapped around a popsicle stick, covered with glue and rolled in glitter. "M" words to emphasize are: metamorphic, mean, midair, meeeeooow, my, mother, marching, music, Mom, midst, missed, mutters.

Experience-based Chart Story: Magic Trick

MATERIALS: 5" × 8" index cards, scissors.
PREPARATION: Practice cutting the index card in the manner indicated below. It is important to make the end cuts first.
PROCEDURE: Say, "Boys and girls, I bet I can fit [child's name] through this card." Hold up the card. Wait for reaction. Follow these steps: (1) Fold the card in half lengthwise. (2) Make about fifteen to twenty cuts, spaced about the width of a finger apart across the card from the folded edge. Stop each cut before the outside edge. (3) Turn the card over and make more cuts in between the first cuts, being careful to stop short of the folded edge. (4) Open the card carefully. (5) Cut the centerfold line, being careful not to cut the top and bottom ends. (6) Without tearing, open out the card until you produce a space large enough to pass over the child's head and body.

Distribute index cards and scissors. Have the children practice the trick. This would be a good opportunity for older children to help out with the cutting. Have the children perform the trick for another group of children.

After the group has gathered in front of the chart paper, ask them to dictate a recounting of their experiences performing the magic trick. Add your own sentences to include "M" words. In the days that follow, read and reread the chart story with your group. Hang it on a chart rack so it is available to the children for their reading enjoyment as their reading skills and strategies improve throughout the year.

As an alternative, distribute language experience paper. Have your group draw pictures about the magic tricks and write scribble stories. Encourage them to include whatever letters they now know how to write. Have them dictate their scribble story to a "secretary" (you, an older student, a parent, a volunteer).

Sound of the Letter Activity: Sorting Objects

MATERIALS: Have on hand objects that begin with "M." Suggestions are: a toy mouse, match, a toy monkey, magazine, magnet, marshmallows, menorah, mirror, mitten, mug, minaret, moccasin, mushroom, and mop. Have a set of objects that do not begin with "M." Miniature objects that can be purchased at toy, hobby, and craft stores may be added to your collection.

PROCEDURE: Have the children sort the items into two piles: one for items that start with "M" and one for items that do not start with "M."

Letter Identification Activity

MATERIALS: Miniature marshmallows, construction paper, glue.
PROCEDURE: Have the children construct the letter "M" by gluing miniature marshmallows to tag board. Tell the children to trace the letter "M" with their fingers. Have them place this page in their key ring alphabet binder.

Play with Language

Have your children sing and dance "The Muffin Man," which can be accessed at www .kididdles.com.

Poem

Lee, Dennis. "The Muddy Puddle." In *The Random House Book of Poetry for Children,* selected by Jack Prelutsky. 1983. Illustrated by Arnold Lobel. New York: Random House. p. 28.

Supplementary Books

Duquette, Keith. 2004. *Cock-a-Doodle Moooo: A Mixed-Up Menagerie.* New York: Putnam.

Flanders, Michael, & Donald Swann. 1991. *The Hippopotamus Song*. Illustrated by Nadine Bernard Westcott. New York: Little, Brown.

Fleming, Candace, & G. Brian Karas. 2002. *Muncha! Muncha! Muncha!* New York: Atheneum Books.

Koller, Jackie French. 1999. *One Monkey Too Many*. Illustrated by Lynn Munsinger. San Diego: Harcourt Brace.

Ogburn, Jacqueline K. 1994. *The Masked Maverick*. Illustrated by Nancy Carlson. New York: Lothrop, Lee & Shepard Books.

Paul, Ann Whitford. 2003. *Little Monkey Says Good Night*. Illustrated by David Walker. New York: Farrar, Straus & Giroux.

Plourde, Lynn. 2004. *Mother, May I?* Illustrated by Amy Wummer. New York: Dutton Children's Books.

Your Ideas

Use this space to record your own ideas for books, materials, and activities.

N

Learning the Letter "N"

Read Aloud

Ehlert, Lois. 1993. *Nuts to You.* San Diego: Harcourt Brace Jovanovich.

☙

A rambunctious squirrel intrigues the narrator, who observes his antics. Ehlert's brilliantly colored collages attract the reader's eye. Be sure to allow the children time to savor Ehlert's illustrations.

Read Aloud to Emphasize the Sound of "N"

Read aloud a second time to emphasize the sound of "N." The word "nuts" appears six times.

Experience-based Chart Story: Filled Nut Cookies

MATERIALS: Chart paper, marker, utensils, ingredients for filled nut-shaped cookies (recipe given at the end of this lesson), tabletop oven. Nut cookie molds (available from The Baker's Catalogue. P.O. Box 876. Norwich VT, O5055-0876. www.kingarthurflour.com). As an alternative, use a nut-shaped or tear-shaped cookie cutter.

PREPARATION: Gather together the utensils, ingredients, cookie cutters or molds, and tabletop oven. Make the filling and have ready. Have an activity ready to go for the half hour it will take for the cookies to cool.

PROCEDURE: With the children taking part or observing, make and bake the filled nut cookies. It would be best to do this in pairs or triads, with help from adult volunteers.

After the cookie baking experience, gather the group in front of the chart paper and ask them to recount what occurred. On the chart paper write the group's recounting. Add your own sentences to include "N" words. In the days that follow, read and reread the chart story with your group. Hang it on a chart rack so it is available to the children for their reading enjoyment as their reading skills and strategies improve throughout the year.

As an alternative, distribute language experience paper. Have your group draw pictures about the races and write scribble stories. Encourage them to include whatever letters they now know how to write. Have them dictate their scribble story to a "secretary" (you, an older student, a parent, a volunteer).

Sound of the Letter Activity: Gathering Nuts Bulletin Board

MATERIALS: Construction paper, brown kraft paper. In addition, have pictures of items that begin with "N," such as nickel, nut, nose, note, neck, necklace, nine, noodles. Pictures may be gathered from the Phonemic Awareness Picture File and other sources of pictures such as coloring books, magazines, Web sites for pictures, phonics workbooks, and catalogs.

PREPARATION: Draw and cut out nut shapes from construction paper. Construct a bulletin board depicting a thirty-six-inch tall squirrel and a basket. By free hand, draw a large squirrel on brown kraft paper. Cut out and attach the squirrel to the bulletin board. Next to the squirrel draw a basket.

PROCEDURE: Have the children glue the pictures of items that begin with "N" to the nut shapes. Have them attach the construction paper nuts to the basket.

Letter Identification Activity

MATERIALS: Tag board, glue, nutshells (be cautious of children's allergies if you use peanuts).

PROCEDURE: Have the children make a large letter "N" on the tag board with glue and adhere the nutshells to the "N" shape. Have the children trace the "N" with their fingers. Tell them to place this page in their key ring alphabet binders.

Play with Language

Have the children learn and sing the old traditional campfire song "I'm a Little Acorn Brown." In *The Complete Book of Rhymes, Songs, Poems, Fingerplays, and Chants,* compiled by Jackie Silberg & Pam Schiller. 2002. Illustrated by Deborah C. Wright. Beltsville, MD: Gryphon House. p. 209.

Poems

Hoberman, Mary Ann. 1998. "Nuts to You." *The Llama Who Had No Pajama.* Illustrated by Betty Fraser. San Diego: Harcourt Brace. p. 19.

Mayer, Gerda. "Noah." In *The Oxford Treasury of Children's Poems,* compiled by Michael Harrison & Christopher Stuart-Clark. 1988. New York: Oxford University Press. p. 78.

Supplementary Books

Hayes, Geoffrey. 2004. *Night-Light for Bunny.* New York: HarperCollins.

London, Jonathan. 1996. *What Newt Could Do for Turtle.* Illustrated by Louise Voce. Cambridge, MA: Candlewick Press.

Lueen, Nancy. 1990. *Nessa's Fish.* Illustrated by Neil Woldman. New York: Atheneum Books for Young Readers.

Root, Phyllis. 1996. *Aunt Nancy and Old Man Trouble.* Illustrated by David Parkins. Cambridge, MA: Candlewick Press.

Wells, Rosemary. 1997. *Noisy Nora.* New York: Dial Books for Young Readers.

Wood, Audrey. 1984. *The Napping House.* Illustrated by Don Wood. San Diego: Harcourt Brace.

Filled Nut-shaped Cookies

Sugar Cookie Recipe

1/2 cup butter	1/4 baking powder
3/4 sugar	1 tablespoon milk
1 1/4 flour	1 egg
1/4 teaspoon salt	1/2 teaspoon vanilla

Cream together the butter and sugar. Add egg and vanilla. Mix. Add milk. Sift together and stir in flour, salt, and baking powder. Fill greased cookie molds with one teaspoon of the dough. Place molds on a cookie sheet and bake for about seven minutes in a 375-degree oven. Remove and let cookies cool. Gently release the cookie by tapping the molds. Spread the filling (see recipes below) on one cookie and top with another cookie to make a sandwich. For cookie cutter cookies, chill the dough. Roll out to 1/4 inch thick. Cut with teardrop-shaped or nut-shaped cookie cutters. Prick the tops of the cookies. Place on a greased cookie sheet. Bake in a 375-degree oven for eight to ten minutes. Remove and let cool. Place a slight teaspoon of fruit and nut or chocolate filling on half of the cookies. Cover with the other half. Press the edges together.

Fruit and Nut Filling

3/4 cup raisins	1/3 cup sugar
3/4 cup chopped walnuts or pecans	2 teaspoons flour
1/2 cup water	

Mix together. Cook slowly until thick. Be careful not to let mixture scorch.

Chocolate Filling

1 stick melted margarine	3 cups powdered sugar
2/3 cup cocoa	1/3 cup milk
1 teaspoon vanilla	

Mix ingredients together. Beat until the filling is of a spreading consistency.

Your Ideas

Use this space to record your own ideas for books, materials, and activities.

SHORT

O

Learning the Letter "O" (Short Sound)

Read Aloud

Kalan, Robert. 1995. *Jump Frog Jump.* Illustrated by Byron Barton. New York: Greenwillow Books.

☙

A frog eludes capture in this cumulative story in which the phrase "Jump, frog, jump" is repeated. Children will soon join you with this phrase as you read the book aloud. Byron Barton's bright tropical color illustrations add visual spice to this cheerful tale.

Read Aloud to Emphasize the Sound of Short "O"

Read aloud again. This time rubber band the words that have the short "O" sound. These are: frog, dropped, and pond, which are repeated throughout the story.

Experience-based Chart Story: Group Story

Using the structure of the story, have your group construct a new story by thinking of an animal that hops or jumps, for example, a kangaroo, rabbit, grasshopper, or bird. You and the children construct a chart story together featuring that animal and using the sentence structure of the text. Hang it on a chart rack so it is available to the children for their reading enjoyment as their reading skills and strategies improve throughout the year.

As an alternative, distribute language experience paper. Have your group draw pictures about an animal that hops and write scribble stories. Encourage them to include whatever letters they now know how to write. Have them dictate their scribble story to a "secretary" (you, an older student, a parent, a volunteer).

Sound of the Letter Activity: The Lily Pad Game

MATERIALS: Used rubber shower mats, a heavy-duty utility knife.

PREPARATION: With the knife, cut the rubber shower mats into about twenty lily pad shapes that are slightly bigger than a child's foot. Be sure to use an appropriate cutting surface. Lay the lily pads out in a large circular path so that a child can hop from one pad to the next.

PROCEDURE: A leader calls out strings of words in which some words contain a short "O" sound and others do not. For example: apple, tiger, oatmeal, mop, pickle. The children are instructed to hop to another lily pad when they hear a word with a short "O" sound.

Letter Identification Activity

MATERIALS: O-shaped pasta.

PROCEDURE: Children glue the O-shaped pasta to the tag board on which they have written a very large letter "O." Tell the children to trace the "O" with their fingers. Have them add this page to their key ring alphabet binders.

Play with Language

Have the children dance the Bunny Hop.

Have the children sing the "The Lively Song of the Frog." In *The Round Book: Rounds Kids Love to Sing,* by Margaret Read MacDonald & Winifred Jaeger. 1999. Illustrated by Yvonne LeBrun Davis. North Haven, CT: Linnet Books. p. 19.

Poem

Ciardi, John. "How to Tell the Top of a Hill." In *Sing a Song of Popcorn,* selected by Beatrice Schenk de Regniers, Eva Moore, Mary Michaels White, & Jan Carr. 1988. New York: Scholastic. p. 119.

Supplementary Books

Harshman, Marc, & Bonnie Collins. 1991. *Rocks in My Pockets.* Illustrated by Toni Goffe. New York: Cobblehill Books.

Harvey, Amanda. 2004. *Dog Gone: Starring Otis.* New York: Doubleday Books for Young Readers.

Kolar, Bob. 1997. *Stomp! Stomp!* New York: North-South Books.

Samton, Sheila. 1995. *Frogs in Clogs.* New York: Crown Publishing Group.

Weeks, Sarah. 2002. *Oh My Gosh, Mrs. McNosh.* Illustrated by Nadine Bernard Westcoff. New York: HarperCollins.

Your Ideas

Use this space to record your own ideas for books, materials, and activities.

LONG
O

Learning the Letter "O" (Long Sound)

Read Aloud

Pearson, Tracy Campbell. 1999. *Where Does Joe Go?* New York: Farrar, Straus & Giroux.

☙

Joe has a snack bar that he operates only in the summer. His customers speculate on where he spends his time in the winter. Pearson's illustrations show what the characters are doing while they are speculating as well as what they are thinking. These are related and it's fun to look for the connection. Be sure not to give the ending away.

Read Aloud to Emphasize the Sound of Long "O"

Read aloud a second time. Rubber band the words so the children can easily hear the long "O" sounds. Long "O" words to emphasize include: bones, Jones, Okefenokee, Bodoky.

Experience-based Chart Story: Where Does Joe Go
Bulletin Board

MATERIALS: Chart paper, markers, drawing paper, crayons.
PROCEDURE: Have the children ask, "I wonder, where does Joe go?" The teacher answers, "I think Joe goes to the supermarket and sells bananas." The children in turn respond to the teacher's question, "I wonder where Joe goes." Next, ask the children to draw a picture of where they think Joe goes. Then, have the children dictate a caption for their stories. Construct a bulletin board with the children's drawings and captions.

After the bulletin board is finished, gather the group in front of the chart paper and ask them to recount what occurred. On the chart paper write the group's recounting. The chart story may be similar to the following examples:

Molly says, "I think Joe goes to Paris and paints pictures."

Mike says, "I think Joe goes to the soccer field and plays the goalie."

Add your own sentences to include "O" words. In the days that follow, read and reread the chart story with your group. Hang it on a chart rack so it is available to the children for their reading enjoyment as their reading skills and strategies improve throughout the year.

Sound of the Letter Activity: File Folder Game

MATERIALS: Stickers, rubber stamps, and/or clip art showing famous places, for example, a pyramid, the Seattle Space Needle, Disney World, or the Eiffel Tower. File folders, dice, index cards. From your Phonemic Awareness Picture File and other sources of pictures, find pictures of items that contain long "O" sounds and items that do not contain "O." Possible items for "O" include: boat, coat, grow, toe, broke, snow, hair bow, row, crow, bone, phone, and rose. Game pieces for each player.

PREPARATION: Prepare a stack of index cards that show pictures of items of words that contain the long "O" sound and items that do not contain the long "O" sound. Draw an oval-shaped game path on the inside of an open file folder. Mark off the game path into squares. Indicate a starting and ending point. Adhere pictures (stickers) of famous places on occasional squares along the game path. Have the following directions on hand.

DIRECTIONS: Two to four players may play. Place the shuffled deck of "O" and non-"O" cards in the middle of the game board. The players throw the pair of dice to see who goes first. The player who rolls the lowest number goes first. The first player draws a card from the stack. If the card shows an item that contains a long "O" sound, the player throws the dice to find out how many spaces he or she may move on the game path. If the drawn card does not show a long "O" sound, the card is discarded and the turn goes to the next player. If the player's marker lands on a picture of a place, the player may move ahead one additional space. The play proceeds in this way until one player reaches home. The first player to reach home wins.

PROCEDURE: Play the game with the children until they can play it independently.

Letter Identification Activity

MATERIALS: O-shaped dry cereal, like Cheerios, tag board, glue.

PROCEDURE: Have the children glue the cereal to the tag board on which a large letter "O" has been written. Tell the children to trace the letter with their fingers. Have them place this page in their key ring alphabet binder.

Play with Language

Teach and sing the round "Row, Row, Row, Your Boat." In *The Complete Book of Rhymes, Songs, Poems, Fingerplays, and Chants,* compiled by Jackie Silberg & Pam Schiller. 2002. Illustrated by Deborah C. Wright. New York: Gryphon House. p. 349.

Poem

Hoberman, Mary Ann. 1998. "O Is Open." *The Llama Who Had No Pajama.* Illustrated by Betty Fraser. San Diego: Harcourt Brace. p. 65.

Supplementary Books

Paul, Ann Whitford. 1998. *Hello Toes! Hello Feet!* Illustrated by Nadine Bernard West-cott. New York: DK Publishing.

Peek, Merle. 1999. *Roll Over.* Boston: Brilliance/Houghton Mifflin. Book and recording kit.

Peterson, Jeanne Whitehorse. 1994. *My Mama Sings.* Illustrated by Sandra Speidel. New York: HarperCollins.

Polacco, Patricia. 2004. *Oh, Look!* New York: Philomel Books.

Shiefman, Vicky. 1994. *Sunday Pototoes. Monday Potatoes.* Illustrated by Louis August. New York: Simon & Schuster Books for Young Readers.

Your Ideas

Use this space to record your own ideas for books, materials, and activities.

P

Learning the Letter "P"

Read Aloud

Kellogg, Steven. 2001. *A Penguin Pup for Pinkerton.* New York: Dial Books for Young Readers.

ơʒ

That perennial favorite chaos-producing Great Dane, Pinkerton, has gotten it into his head that a football is a penguin egg, one that he must hatch no matter what. In the course of this effort, Pinkerton causes havoc. Granny comes up with a clever solution and saves Pinkerton from imminent arrest. Be sure to allow the children time to enjoy this thoroughly comedic illustrated tale. Draw their attention to the second story taking place in the dreams of Rose, the cat, and Pinkerton.

Read Aloud to Emphasize the Sound of "P"

Read aloud the second time. Have the children wave little pennants constructed from popsicle sticks and construction paper every time they hear the words that begin with the sound of "P." These words are: Pinkerton, perfect, parent, penguin, parents, poor, patiently, pooch, park, police, pup, Pinkwin. Before reading, tell the children to wave their pennants every time you emphasize the sound of "P."

Experience-based Chart Story: Paper Bag Puppets

MATERIALS: White paper lunch bags, Penguin, girl, man, woman, and dog patterns for paper bag puppets, glue, construction paper. For ideas for patterns, see Web sites for teachers listed in the introduction.

PROCEDURE: Distribute the materials and have the children construct the paper bag puppets. Have the children create an informal puppet show. Give them the opportunity to perform their puppet shows to each other or other groups of children.

After the paper bag puppet shows, gather the group in front of the chart paper and ask them to recount what occurred. On the chart paper write the group's recounting. Add your own sentences to include "P" words. In the days that follow, read and reread the chart story with your group. Hang it on a chart rack so it is available to the children for their reading enjoyment as their reading skills and strategies improve throughout the year.

As an alternative, distribute language experience paper. Have your group draw pictures about their puppet show and write scribble stories. Encourage them to include whatever letters they now know how to write. Have them dictate their scribble story to a "secretary" (you, an older student, a parent, a volunteer).

Sound of the Letter Activity: Antarctica Bulletin Board

MATERIALS: White bulletin board paper, craft sticks, construction paper, sources for pictures, glue, crayons, scissors, stapler, penguin patterns.

PREPARATION: Construct a snowy white bulletin board depicting Antarctica.

PROCEDURE: Distribute penguin patterns, construction paper, crayons, magazines, phonics workbooks, catalogs, coloring books, glue, and scissors to your students. Have the children construct and color their penguin. Using construction paper, craft sticks, and pictures of items that start with "P" have the children create signs. The size of the sign will depend on the size of the picture. Attach the signs to each of the penguins. Attach the sign-carrying penguins to the Antarctica bulletin board scene.

Letter Identification Activity

Pop popcorn. Have the children glue popcorn to the shape of the letter "P" on their tag board. Have them place this page in their key ring alphabet binder.

Play with Language

Recite this tongue twister to your group: "Peter Piper picked a peck of pickled peppers. How many peppers did Peter Piper pick?" Teach the tongue twister to the group. Have them practice saying it.

Poem

Sierra, Judy. 1998. *Antarctic Antics: A Book of Penguin Poems.* Illustrated by Jose Aruego & Ariane Dewey. San Diego: Harcourt Brace.

Supplementary Books

Aldridge, Josephine Haskell. 1994. *The Pocket Book.* Illustrated by Rene King Moreno. New York: Simon & Schuster Books for Young Readers.

Andreae, Giles. 2003. *Pants.* Illustrated by Nick Sharratt. Oxford, UK: David Fickling Books.

Cooper, Helen. 1998. *Pumpkin Soup.* New York: Farrar, Straus & Giroux.

Khalsa, Dayal Kaur. 1989. *How Pizza Came to Queens.* New York: Clarkson N. Potter.

McMillan, Bruce. 1995. *Puffins Climb. Penguins Rhyme.* San Diego: Harcourt Brace.

Palatine, Margie. 1995. *Piggie Pie.* Illustrated by Howard Fine. Boston: Clarion Books.

Van Leeuwen, Jean. 2004. *Oliver the Mighty Pig.* Illustrated by Ann Schweninger. New York: Dial Books for Young Readers.

Your Ideas

Use this space to record your own ideas for books, materials, and activities.

Q

Learning the Letter "Q"

Read Aloud

Thompson, Lauren. 2003. *Little Quack.* Illustrated by Derek Anderson. New York: Simon & Schuster Books for Young Readers.

Little Quack is fearful of jumping out of the nest and into the pond. His family's encouragement helps him overcome his fear. Children will be reassured about overcoming their own fears as they listen to this heartwarming story. The quack-u-lator, rolling along like the CNN news crawl, provides an additional element that turns the text into a counting story. Derek Anderson portrays a duck face everyone can love.

Read Aloud to Emphasize the Sound of "Q"

Read aloud a second time. Before you start, tell your group to wave duck stick puppets whenever they hear the sound of "Q." "Quack" appears on almost every page.

Experience-based Chart Story: Little Quack Quilt

MATERIALS: Chart paper, marker, squares of nonglossy drawing paper, iron, transfer fabric crayons, four-inch squares of white cloth that is not less than 50 percent synthetic for each child in your group, prepared four-inch cloth square depicting Little Quack.

PREPARATION: Supply each child in your group with transfer fabric crayons, a square of synthetic cloth, and squares of nonglossy drawing paper.

PROCEDURE: Have each child draw and color with transfer fabric crayons a picture of an item that begins with "Q" onto the squares of nonglossy paper. Suggestions are: quail, queen, quilt, quack, quarter, quart, quartet, and question. Encourage them to use pressure when coloring. Have a volunteer transfer the child's crayoned drawings onto the cloth squares by ironing them with a dry iron set on the cotton setting. Have the volunteer sew the pieces together so that the Little Quack square is in the middle. Display the Little Quack Quilt in your classroom. Technically, a quilt top has been constructed up to this point. If you wish, you or a volunteer might demonstrate how to construct a quilt complete with a backing, batting, and tacking.

After the group has gathered in front of the chart paper, ask them to recount what occurred. Write the group's recounting of making the quilt. Add your own sentences to ensure that words beginning with "Q" are included in the chart story.

As an alternative, distribute language experience paper. Have the children draw pictures about the quilt construction and write scribble stories. Encourage them to include whatever letters they now know how to write. Have them dictate their scribble story to a "secretary" (you, an older student, a parent, a volunteer).

Sound of the Letter Activity: Using the Quack-u-lator

MATERIALS: From your Phonemic Awareness Picture File and other sources of pictures, find pictures of items that begin with "Q," such as queen, quilt, quadruplets, quetzal, quail, quarrel, quartet, quartz, and question mark, and pictures of items that do not begin with "Q." Construction paper, glue.

PREPARATION: Glue the pictures to construction paper. Five "Q" pictures and five non-"Q" pictures will be enough. As with all phonics and phonemic awareness activities, be sure the children know the names of all the items before the activity begins.

PROCEDURE: Ask the children to count by quacking the number of times "Q" items are shown. For example, the fourth time a "Q" picture is held up the children would answer, "Quack, quack, quack, quack."

Letter Identification Activity

MATERIALS: Scraps of old (not antique) quilts or quilted fabric, tag board, glue.

Have the children write the letter "Q" with glue on poster board. Have them glue old quilt scraps to the letter. Tell the children to trace the letter with their fingers. Have them add this page to their key ring alphabet binder.

Play with Language

Pair up your students with older students who can help them find and explain words that start with "Q" in online and hard copy dictionaries. Have the older children help your children make up alliterative sentences and draw pictures to illustrate them. For example, Queen Quinnie's quiltmaker quoted a quadrupled quantity for quite a quilt.

Poem

Jacobs, Leland. "Queenie." In *The Random House Anthology of Children's Poetry,* selected by Jack Prelutsky. 1983. Illustrated by Arnold Lobel. New York: Random House. p. 109.

Supplementary Books

Cates, Karin. 2002. *A Far-Fetched Story.* Illustrated by Nancy Carpenter. New York: Greenwillow Books.

Cronin, Doreen. 2002. *Giggle, Giggle, Quack.* Illustrated by Betsy Lewin. New York: Simon & Schuster Books for Young Readers.

Gerstein, Mordicai. 2000. *Queen Esther, the Morning Star.* New York: Simon & Schuster Books for Young Readers.

Johnston, Tony. 1985. *The Quilt Story.* Illustrated by Tomie dePaola. New York: G. P. Putnam's Sons.

Root, Phyllis. 2003. *The Name Quilt.* Illustrated by Margot Apple. New York: Farrar, Straus & Giroux.

Your Ideas

Use this space to record your own ideas for books, materials, and activities.

R

Learning the Letter "R"

Read Aloud

Wood, Audrey. 1996. *Red Racer*. New York: Simon & Schuster Books for Young Readers.

❧

Nona dreams of owning a red racer bicycle. She finds inventive ways to get rid of her old clunker but each of her ploys are blocked. Finally, her parents come to her rescue with a practical but satisfying solution. Audrey Wood's digitally illustrated pictures create a humorous addition to her storyline.

Read Aloud to Emphasize the Sound of "R"

Read aloud a second time to emphasize the sound of "R." Have the children wave bicycle stick puppets (a rubber stamp figure of a bicycle glued to a craft stick) whenever they hear the sound of "R." Words that begin with "R" in this book are: right, rang, road, rolled, ran, rest, railroad, and raced.

Experience-based Chart Story: RRRRaces

MATERIALS: Chart paper, markers. radishes, spoons, jump ropes, sacks. There are all types of races. Have enough variety so that every child or pair has a chance to win.
Here are some ideas:

Red Radish on a Spoon Race

Hop Like Rabbits Race

Jumping Rope Race

Hop on One Foot Race

Linked Arms Back to Back Race

Sack Race

Divide the group into pairs or teams and assign them names that start with "R," such as Radish Racers, Roaring Rabbits, Roping Runners, and Ruddy Ropers. Conduct the races. Distribute prizes.

After the group has gathered in front of the chart paper, ask them to recount what occurred. On the chart paper write the group's recounting. Add your own sentence to include "R" words. In the days that follow, read and reread the chart story with your group.

As an alternative, distribute language experience paper. Have your group draw pictures about the races and write scribble stories. Encourage them to include whatever letters they now know how to write. Have them dictate their scribble story to a "secretary" (you, an older student, a parent, a volunteer).

Sound of the Letter Activity: Three Ring Spin

MATERIALS: Glue, scissors, a wooden dowel (a wooden cooking spoon works nicely) for each child, a cardboard tube (toilet paper tube for each child), three to five small pictures of items that begin with "R," such as ring, rose, ribbon, rug, roller blades, rock, or rope, and four to six pictures of items that do not begin with "R."

PREPARATION: Cut the cardboard tube into three sections (rings). Glue three to five "R" pictures and the other pictures in an evenly spaced manner around the cardboard rings. String the rings onto the wooden dowel/spoon.

PROCEDURE: Distribute the devices to each child. Instruct the children to flip each of the three cardboard rings with their fingers so that the three rings spin. When the rings stop spinning have the children declare whether or not they have three "R" pictures in a row. Award a point to those who do. Repeat. At the end of ten or so spins, count the points. Give each child a reward for each of their accumulated points.

Letter Identification Activity

MATERIALS: Raisins, glue, tag board.

PROCEDURE: Have the children write a large letter "R" on the tag board and then glue raisins to the outline. Coat the raisins with Mod Podge or paint with clear nail polish. Have the children add these tag board pages to their key ring alphabet binders.

Play with Language

Teach and have the children recite the tongue twister "Robert Rowley Rolled a Round." In *The Complete Book of Rhymes, Songs, Poems, Fingerplays, and Chants,* compiled by Jackie Silberg & Pam Schiller. 2002. Illustrated by Deborah C. Wright. Beltsville, MD: Gryphon House. p. 343.

Poem

Ciardi, John. "Rain Sizes." In *V Is for Verses,* by Odille Ousley. Boston: Ginn & Co. 1967. (Also available on several sites on the Internet.)

Supplementary Books

Carlstrom, Nancy White. 1997. *Raven and the River*. Illustrated by Jon Van Zyle. New York: Little, Brown.

Compestine, Ying Chang. 2001. *The Runaway Rice Cake*. Illustrated by Tungwai Chau. New York: Simon & Schuster Books for Young Readers.

Kalan, Robert. 1978. *Rain*. Illustrated by Donald Crews. New York: Greenwillow Books.

Kurtz, Jane. 2002. *Rain Romp*. Illustrated by Dyanna Wolcott. New York: Greenwillow Books.

Wood, Audrey. 1993. *Rude Giants*. San Diego: Harcourt Brace.

Your Ideas

Use this space to record your own ideas for books, materials, and activities.

S

Learning the Letter "S"

Read Aloud

Bunting, Eve. 1996. *Sunflower House.* Illustrated by Kathryn Hewitt. San Diego: Harcourt Brace.

Ω

In rhyming text a little boy recounts the sequence of events when he plants a sunflower house. After his dad digs out a circle in the lawn, the boy plants seeds and watches as a sunflower house grows. He and his friends play in it all summer long. They even sleep in it one moonlit night. When autumn comes, they collect the seeds.

Read Aloud to Emphasize the Sound of "S"

Read aloud a second time. Have the children wave sunflower stick puppets (Simple construction paper sunflower-shapes glued to a craft stick) whenever they hear a word that begins with "S." Words that begin with "S" are: says, say, see, songs, sunflowers, seeds, set, secret, some something, super-duper, such, summer.

Experience-based Chart Story: Sunflower House

MATERIALS: Chart paper, marker, sunflower seeds, garden tools, weed barrier cloth.

PROCEDURE: After the danger of frost is past, have volunteers and your children dig a circular plot about five feet in diameter in a spot that gets at least six hours of sunshine each day. Lay down weed barrier cloth in a circular shape about four feet in diameter. Secure with rocks, spikes, or plastic earth nails. Have the children plant sunflower seeds six to eight inches apart around the outside edge of the weed barrier cloth. Leave about an eighteen-inch space for an entrance to the sunflower house. Water and fertilize. Over the summer keep watering, weeding, and fertilizing. Place child-sized chairs, pillows, and books inside the sunflower house.

In northern climates, sunflowers may be started by planting sunflower seeds in milk cartons eight weeks before the end of frost date or purchased from local nursery. Check with local garden clubs to find out about financial support through grants. If a plot of ground is not available, consider growing the sunflowers in barrels placed in a circle.

At various times throughout this project, gather the children in front of chart paper and have them recount their experiences so that you have a progress record. Post the chart paper recountings where the children can read them repeatedly.

Sound of the Letter Activity: Sunflower Catch

MATERIALS: Garden gloves, yellow felt, Velcro circles, a basket of tennis balls.
PREPARATION: On the palm side of the garden gloves, glue yellow felt petals in a circle similar to a sunflower. Glue a Velcro circle in the middle.
PROCEDURE: Have a child wear one of the gloves. Toss a tennis ball to the child and have the child say a word that begins with "S." The aim of this activity is to have the child say a word that begins with "S" while catching the tennis ball. This activity can be done in teams, or one on one, depending on the size of your group.

Letter Identification Activity

MATERIALS: Tag board, glue, pencils with erasers, yellow crepe paper or tissue paper cut into ½-inch squares, small plastic or paper cup to hold the glue.
PROCEDURE: Have each child print a large letter "S" on his or her poster board. Have them twist a square of paper around the eraser end of the pencil, dip the end of the pencil into the glue, and press the glued yellow paper along the lines of the letter.

After the glue has dried, have them trace over the letter with the index finger of their writing hand. Have them place this page in their alphabet key ring binder.

As an alternative, have children glue down sunflower seeds instead of paper squares.

Play with Language.

Learn the Appalachian folktale "Sody Sallyaratus." As you tell the story, invite the children to join you in repeating the chant "Sody, sody, sody sallyaratus." Source: Freeman, Barbara, & Connie Regan-Blake. *Tales to Grow On.* Norwalk, CT: Weston Woods. Audiotape.

Poem

Justus, May. "The Rain Has Silver Sandals." In *The Random House Book of Poetry for Children,* selected by Jack Prelutsky. 1983. Illustrated by Arnold Lobel. New York: Random House. p. 29.

Supplementary Books

Ernst, Lisa Campbell. 2004. *Wake Up, It's Spring.* New York: HarperCollins.
Gray, Libba Moore. 1996. *Little Lil and the Swing-Singing Sax.* 1996. Illustrated by Lisa Cohen. New York: Simon & Schuster Books for Young Readers.

Sloat, Teri. 1997. *Sody Sallyratus.* New York: Dutton Children's Books.
Wood, Audrey. 1992. *Silly Sally.* San Diego: Harcourt Brace.

Your Ideas

Use this space to record your own ideas books, materials, and activities.

T

Learning the Letter "T"

Read Aloud

Hague, Michael. 1993. *Teddy Bear, Teddy Bear.* New York: William Morrow.

ଔ

Michael Hague's child-appealing illustrations portray a charming teddy bear doing the activities described in the traditional action rhyme. Children are invited to do the actions.

Read Aloud to Emphasize the Sound of "T"

Read the story again and have the children do the actions. While the children are doing the actions, put a special emphasis on the "T" words. Words beginning with "T" in addition to teddy bear are turn, touch, and turn off.

Experience-based Chart Story: Teddy Bear Tea Party

MATERIALS: Chart paper, marker, teddy bears, teddy bear-shaped cookies, punch, paper plates, cups.

PREPARATION: Invite the children to bring in their teddy bears and other stuffed animals to a tea party. For children who are without a teddy bear, have teddy bears on hand. Inexpensive ones can be purchased from second-hand stores such as Goodwill or St. Vincent's. Ask volunteers to make punch and cookies and to help serve.

After the teddy bear tea party is over, have the children gather in front of the chart paper. Have them dictate a recounting of the experience. Include your own sentences to guarantee "T" words.

As an alternative, distribute language experience paper. Have your group draw pictures about the teddy bear tea party and write scribble stories. Encourage them to include whatever letters they now know how to write. Have them dictate their scribble story to a "secretary" (you, an older student, a parent, a volunteer).

Sound of the Letter Activity: "T" Scene Bulletin Board

MATERIALS: White bulletin board paper, markers, pictures of items that begin with the sound of "T" from your Phonemic Awareness Picture File and other sources of pictures such as catalogs, Web sites for pictures, phonics workbooks, magazines, coloring books, and clip art. Suggestions are: teapot, tree, tomato, train, tee shirt, tee (golf), television, telephone, tire, toad, toast, towel, tulip.

PREPARATION: On the bulletin board draw a horizon line, a house, and human figures.

PROCEDURE: Have the children cut out and/or draw pictures of items that begin with "T" to place on the bulletin board scene. Tell them to review the pictures and say the names of the items in their free time. This could be done in pairs and small groups with one child playing the role of teacher who points to the objects.

Letter Identification Activity

MATERIALS: Tag board, glue, scrap pieces of fake fur cut into $1/2$-inch squares.

PROCEDURE: Have the children write a large letter "T" on the tag board. Have them glue the fake fur cloth scraps onto the "T" shape. Have the children trace the letter and tell them to include this page in their alphabet key ring binder.

Play with Language

Have the children jump rope and chant the teddy bear jump rope rhyme in *Anna Banana,* compiled by Joanna Cole. Illustrated by Alan Tiegreen. p. 36. New York: Morrow Junior Books. 1989.

Poem

Hoberman, Mary Ann. 1998. "Timothy Toppin." *The Llama Who Had No Pajama.* Illustrated by Betty Fraser. San Diego: Harcourt Brace. p. 39.

Supplementary Books

Bowie, C. W. 1998. *Busy Toes.* Illustrated by Fred Willingham. Dallas, TX: Whispering Coyote Press.

Hutchins, Pat. 1991. *Tidy Titch.* New York: Greenwillow Books.

Olson, Mary W. 2000. *Nice Try Tooth Fairy.* Illustrated by Katherine Tillotson. New York: Simon & Schuster Books for Young Readers.

O'Malley, Kevin. 1999. *Leo Cockroach . . . Toy Tester.* New York: Walker & Co.

Soto, Gary. 1992. *Too Many Tamales.* Illustrated by Ed Martinez. New York: The Putnam & Grosset Group.

Your Ideas

Use this space to record your own ideas for books, materials, and activities.

SHORT
U

Learning the Letter "U" (Short Sound)

Read Aloud

Wheeler, Lisa. 2004. *Bubble Gum, Bubble Gum.* Illustrated by Laura Huliska-Beith. New York: Little, Brown.

ಐ

The trouble all started with an icky piece of bubble gum stuck in the middle of the road. As in the Tar Baby folktale, it attracts an animal to become stuck on it. Unlike the Tar Baby, five animals, not just one, become stuck. Wheeler's lively language combined with Huliska-Beith's colorful collages result in a book that children will ask to hear repeatedly.

Read Aloud to Emphasize the Sound of Short "U"

Read aloud the second time. Words to emphasize are: bubble, gum, yuck, stuck, bumpy, grumpy, buzz, bumbled, bumble, grumble, stumble, gum-feathered, truck, luck, ruffled.

Experience-based Chart Story: Thumbprint Pictures

MATERIALS: Chart paper, markers, ink pads, paper, pens, *Ed Emberley's Great Thumbprint Book* (1977, Boston: Little, Brown), and an example of a thumbprint creature.

PROCEDURE: Distribute pens, paper, and inkpads to the children. Show the children the thumbprint book and your example of a thumbprint creature. Have the children press their thumbs onto the inkpad and then onto the paper. Have them make thumbprint illustrations of the animals that got stuck in the bubble gum blob.

After making thumbprint pictures, gather the group in front of the chart paper. Ask them to recount what occurred. On the chart paper write the group's recounting. Add your own sentences to include short "U" words. In the days that follow, read and reread the chart story with your group. Hang it on a chart rack so it is available to the children for their reading enjoyment as their reading skills and strategies improve throughout the year.

As an alternative, distribute language experience paper. Have your group construct thumbprint pictures about the *Bubble Gum, Bubble Gum* story and write scribble stories. Encourage them to include whatever letters they now know how to write. Have them dictate their scribble story to a "secretary" (you, an older student, a parent, a volunteer).

Sound of the Letter Activity: Thumbs Up

MATERIALS: Pictures of items that do not contain the short "U" sound and pictures of short "U" items. These may be: mug, nut, tub, hut, sun, bun, bug, rug, cup, up, buck, truck, gum, thumb, fudge, trudge, cut, mutt. Catalogs, magazines, Web sites for pictures, coloring books, clip art, and phonics workbooks as well as your Phonemic Awareness Picture File are good sources for pictures.

PROCEDURE: Play a Thumbs Up game. Show the children a mix of pictures of items that contain the short "U" sound and some that do not. Have the children give a thumbs up sign whenever you show a picture of an item that represents the short "U" sound.

Letter Identification Activity

MATERIALS: Prepared chocolate pudding, finger painting paper, newspaper, water.

PREPARATION: Be sure parents are alerted that this is a messy activity and children will need a painting smock (a very large T-shirt or an old shirt). Have helpers on hand. Distribute the finger painting paper. Plop about two tablespoons of chocolate pudding on each sheet of paper.

PROCEDURE: Have the children finger paint the letter "U" over all their papers. Clean up. Allow the finger paintings to dry. Have the children place their fingerpaintings in their key ring alphabet binders.

Play with Language

Have your children jump rope to the bubble gum jump rope rhyme in *Anna Banana,* compiled by Joanna Cole. 1989. Illustrated by Alan Tiegren. New York: Morrow Junior Books. p. 38.

Poem

Lee, Dennis. "The Muddy Puddle." In *The Random House Book of Poetry,* selected by Jack Prelutsky. 1983. Illustrated by Arnold Lobel. New York: Random House. p. 28.

Supplementary Books

Alborough, Jez. 1993. *Cuddly Dudley.* Cambridge, MA: Candlewick Press.
Butler, John. 2002. *Hush, Little Ones.* Atlanta, GA: Peachtree Publishers.
Buzzeo, Toni. 2003. *Dawdle Duckling.* Illustrated by Margaret Spengler. New York: Dial Books for Young Readers.
Collier Bryan. 2000. *Uptown.* New York: Henry Holt.

Plourde, Lynn. 1997. *Pigs in the Mud in the Middle of the Rud.* Illustrated by John Schoenherr. New York: Blue Sky Press.

Webb, Steve. 2003. *Tanka Tanka Skunk.* New York: Orchard Books.

Your Ideas

Use this space to record your own ideas for books, materials, and activities.

LONG

U

Learning the Letter "U" (Long Sound)

Read Aloud

Bogan, Paulette. 2003. *Goodnight Lulu*. London: Bloomsbury Children's Books.

↺

Keep your eyes on the pigs! Bogan's animated drawings of a timid chicken, her exasperated mother, and some opportunistic pigs make for a delightful, humorous story that children are sure to ask to be repeated. Children will identify with the little chicken's bedtime fears. They will also get a kick out of the secondary story happening as the pigs eavesdrop on the mother's reassurances and slyly move their way toward the bed covers.

Read Aloud to Emphasize the Sound of the Letter "U"

Read aloud the second time. Long "U" words are admittedly scarce; however, "Lulu" appears on several pages throughout the story. Focus on them by rubber banding the "U" sound.

Experience-based Chart Story: Blue "Gluep" Constructions

MATERIALS: Chart paper, marker, liquid starch, rock salt, white glue, dry blue tempera paint, disposable mixing bowl (such as a plastic gallon jug with the top cut off), mixing stick, and a pieces of heavy cardboard for each child.

PREPARATION: Mix together ½ cup liquid starch, 2 cups rock salt, ½ cup white glue, blue tempera paint.

PROCEDURE: Divide the blue "gluep" by plopping it onto each child's heavy cardboard. Have the children experiment constructing forms of any sort from this clay. It dries hard. Have the children give their objects real or silly names as appropriate.

After playing with blue "gluep," gather the group in front of the chart paper. Ask them to recount what occurred. Add your own sentences to include long "U" words. In the days that follow, read and reread the chart story with your group. Hang it on a chart rack so it is available to the children for their reading enjoyment as their reading skills and strategies improve throughout the year.

As an alternative, distribute language experience paper. Have your group draw pictures about their blue "gluep" experience and write scribble stories. Encourage them to include whatever letters they now know how to write. Have them dictate their scribble story to a "secretary" (you, an older student, a parent, a volunteer).

Sound of the Letter Activity: Saving the Blue Unicorn Game

MATERIALS: A used stuffed toy unicorn with a blue ribbon tied around its neck, 5" × 8" index cards with holes punched in the top left and right corner, yarn, glue, and pictures of items that contain the long "U" sound from your Phonemic Awareness Picture File and other sources of pictures. Pictures of items that contain the long "U" sound are: flute, glue, prune, cucumber, tuba, tube, soup, plume, juice, ukulele, suit. A list of words that have the long "U" sound include: cute, mute, clue, flute, lute, blue, flue, hue, true, due, glue, tune, dune, prune, duke, fume, plume, juice, use, fuse, muse, dude, rude, ukulele, use, suit, cube, cucumber, tube, tuba.

PREPARATION: Thread the yarn through the holes in the cards so as to make a loop and knot it to make it secure. Glue pictures on the index cards so that two cards will have the same picture.

PROCEDURE: Tell the children to form a wide circle. Place the blue unicorn in the middle of the circle. Distribute the picture cards to the children to hang around their necks. Be sure they know what word the picture represents. Tell the children that you will call out a word. Tell them that if their picture matches the word that is called, they should run to the center, grab the unicorn, and shout, "I saved the blue unicorn" and score a point. Call out pairs of words, some of which match the pictures, such as "flute" and "cucumber," and some of which do not, such as "cute" and "flue."

Letter Identification Activity: Frozen Dough Letters

MATERIALS: Greased cookie sheets, frozen dough from the market, egg white, cinnamon, sugar.

PROCEDURE: Have the children shape thawed dough into "U" shapes. Brush with egg white and sprinkle with cinnamon sugar. Bake twenty minutes in a 350-degree oven. Eat and enjoy. Have the children glue one of the letter "U"s to tag board and place it in their key ring alphabet binder after brushing with Mod Podge.

Play with Language

Teach and sing the song "Alouette." In *The Complete Book of Rhymes, Songs, Poems, Fingerplays, and Chants,* compiled by Jackie Silberg & Pam Schiller. 2002. Illustrated by Deborah C. Wright. Beltsville, MD: Gryphon House. pp. 18–19.

Poem

Hoban, Russell. "Stupid Old Myself." In *The Random House Poetry for Children,* selected by Jack Prelutsky. 1983. Illustrated by Arnold Lobel. New York: Random House. p. 125.

Supplementary Books

Low, Alice. 2004. *Aunt Lucy Went to Buy a Hat.* Illustrated by Laura Huliska-Beith. New York: HarperCollins.
McCloskey, Robert. 1948. *Blueberries for Sal.* New York: Viking Press.
Teague, Mark. 2002. *Dear Mrs. LaRue.* New York: Scholastic.
Uff, Caroline. 2000. *Lulu's Busy Day.* New York: Walker & Co.
Wood, Audrey. 1993. *Rude Giants.* San Diego: Harcourt Brace.

Your Ideas

Use this space to record your own ideas for books, materials, and activities.

V

Learning the Letter "V"

Read Aloud

Eclare, Melanie. 2002. *A Harvest of Color: Growing a Vegetable Garden.* Brooklyn, NY: Ragged Bears.

ℂℽ

Five children introduce the reader to the vegetables they grew in their garden. Eclare captures their thoughtful and happy faces in her color photographs. Each child provides the reader with tips for growing each vegetable. A recipe for vegetable salad is given at the end.

Read Aloud to Emphasize the Sound of "V"

The letter "V" appears several times within the text. Be sure to rubber band the sound of "V" when it occurs. Ask the children, "What are zucchini, carrots, potatoes, green beans, and radishes?" in order to elicit "V" one more time.

Experience-based Chart Story: Vegetable Salad

MATERIALS: Chart paper and marker. The recipe given at the end of *A Harvest of Color: Growing a Vegetable Garden.* Zucchini, potatoes, radishes, green beans, carrots, water, salad dressing or vinegar and olive oil, salt and pepper, mustard. Chopping board, knife, vegetable steamer, pan, hot plate or stove, mixing bowl, wisk, plates, forks.

PREPARATION: Chop the vegetables into bite-sized pieces. Steam the green beans and zucchini. Cool. Boil the potatoes until tender. Cool and dice.

PROCEDURE: Have the children help make the salad or observe an adult making it. Have the children make the salad dressing by mixing the vinegar, olive oil, salt, pepper, and mustard, or use a prepared salad dressing. Place all the cooled, chopped vegetables in a bowl and pour salad dressing over all. Serve the vegetable salad and enjoy.

As an alternative, plant a vegetable garden or plant a large half barrel with vegetables.

After the group has gathered in front of the chart paper, ask them to recount what occurred. On the chart paper write the group's recounting, Add your own sentences to include "V" words.

As an alternative, distribute language experience paper. Have your group draw pictures about making vegetable salad or planting the vegetable garden and write scribble stories. Encourage them to include whatever letters they now know how to write. Have them dictate their scribble story to a "secretary" (you, an older student, a parent, a volunteer).

Sound of the Letter Activity: Drawing "V" Pictures

MATERIALS: Items that begin with "V," such as a bottle of vanilla, a vanilla bean, vinegar, valentines, velvet, a vine, a violet plant, vest, volleyball, violin, and vegetables. Drawing paper, crayons.

PREPARATION: Place an assortment of the items on display on a table in front of the group of children.

PROCEDURE: Pick up each item and tell the children what each item is, emphasizing the beginning sound. Allow them to touch and explore each item. After they have explored the items, have them pick one to draw and color with crayons. Display their drawings on a bulletin board. Ask them what a good title for the bulletin board might be.

Letter Identification Activity

MATERIALS: Scraps of velvet, glue, tag board.

PROCEDURE: Have the children write a large "V" on their tag board. Have them glue velvet scraps to the "V" outline. Have them place this page in their key ring alphabet binders.

Play with Language

Have the children sing the chorus to "The Happy Wanderer." Lyrics may be accessed from www.scoutsongs.com.

Have the children sing the round "Viva, Viva la Musica." In *The Round Book: Rounds Kids Love to Sing,* by Margaret Read MacDonald & Winifred Jaeger. 1999. Illustrated by Yvonne LeBrun Davis. North Haven, CT: Linnet Books. p. 8.

Poem

McNaughton, Colin. 1987. "Tracy Venables." In *There's an Awful Lot of Weirdoes in Our Neighborhood.* Cambridge, MA: Candlewick Press. p. 53.

Supplementary Books

Best, Cari. 2001. *Shrinking Violet.* Illustrated by Giselle Potter. New York: Farrar, Straus & Giroux.

De Groat, Diane. 1996. *Roses Are Pink, Your Feet Really Stink.* New York: Morrow Junior Books.

Donohue, Dorothy. 2000. *Veggie Soup.* New York: Winslow Press.

Funke, Cornelia. 2004. *The Princess Knight*. Illustrated by Kerstin Meyer. New York: Scholastic.

Johnson, Angela. 2004. *Violet's Music*. Illustrated by Laura Huliska-Beith. New York: Dial Books for Young Readers.

O'Malley, Kevin. 1997. *Velcome*. New York: Walker & Co.

Pinkwater, Daniel. 1991. *Wempires*. New York: Macmillan.

Voake, Charlotte. 1992. "Mr. Vinegar." In *The Three Little Pigs and Other Favorite Nursery Stories*. Cambridge, MA: Candlewick Press.

Your Ideas

Use this space to record your own ideas for books, materials, and activities.

Learning the Letter "W"

Read Aloud

Appelt, Kathi. 1996. *A Red Wagon Year.* Illustrated by Laura McGee Kvasnosky. San Diego: Harcourt Brace.

慘

Laura McGee Kvanosky's colorful, endearing illustrations depict the story of six children as they use a red wagon for various purposes each month. For example, in January the children fill it with bird seed and use it as a feeder, in July they use it for a float in the Fourth of July parade, and in October they decorate it as a space ship for Halloween trick or treating. Young children can learn the months of the year as they enjoy looking at this set of charming illustrations.

If you cannot locate *A Red Wagon Year,* I recommend that you read *Diary of a Worm,* by Doreen Cronin, and start a worm farm raising red wiggler worms as the experience.

Read Aloud to Emphasize the Sound of "W"

Have the children browse through the pictures in the book a second time. Draw their attention to items or actions in the illustrations that depict words that begin with "W." For example: January—winter, wagon, wings, watching. February—wagon, walk, wag, waiting. March—wagon, wind, weathervane, window. April—wagon, warm. May—wagon, wooden (the fence), words (on the sign). June—wave, water. July—wave, wing, winging. August—wash, wet, warm, watering can, water. September—wave, weep, walk. October—witch, waist, wide-eyed, watchful, wig. November—wall, walk, wear (a hat), wide (scarecrow's arm spread). December—watching, waiting.

Experience-based Chart Story: Wagon Train

MATERIALS: Chart paper, markers, tape player/CD player, audiotape/CD of "The March of the Toy Soldiers," wagons, used toys and books that have been approved by the children to be given away.

PREPARATION: Plan ahead to be sure that each child in the younger class will have a toy and/or book.

PROCEDURE: Have a wagon parade. Have the children load their wagons with used toys and books to parade to a kindergarten or pre-kindergarten class. Make one wagon the music wagon and play "The March of the Toy Soldiers" as you march along. Have your children distribute the toys and/or books to the younger children.

After the group has gathered in front of the chart paper, ask them to recount what occurred. On the chart paper write the group's recounting. Add your own sentence to include "W" words. In the days that follow, read and reread the chart story with your group.

As an alternative, distribute language experience paper. Have your group draw pictures about the wagon parade and write scribble stories. Encourage them to include whatever letters they now know how to write. Have them dictate their scribble story to a "secretary" (you, an older student, a parent, a volunteer).

Sound of the Letter Study: "W" Windows

MATERIALS: Glue, clear tape, clear plastic wrap, and a 9" × 12" piece of construction paper for each child. From your Phonemic Awareness Picture File and other sources, obtain pictures of items that begin with "W" such as: wig, wallpaper, wagon, web, witch, wall, watch, waffle, wallet, walrus, walnuts, window, wolf.

PREPARATION: Cut a 7" × 10" rectangle out of the center of the construction paper so that a frame is formed.

PROCEDURE: Help the children tape or glue the clear plastic wrap onto the construction paper frame. Have the children glue a picture of a "W" item in the middle the clear plastic wrap. Display the children's "W" windows in a classroom window.

Letter Identification Activity

MATERIALS: Wallpaper samples, tag board, glue.

PROCEDURE: Have the children write a large letter "W" on their tag boards. Have them tear pieces of wallpaper and glue them to the letter. Have them add this page to their key ring alphabet binders.

Play with Language

Teach and have the children sing the round "Wake up. Wake up." In *The Round Book: Rounds Kids Love to Sing,* by Margaret Read MacDonald & Winifred Jaeger. 1999. Illustrated by Yvonne LeBrun Davis. North Haven, CT: Linnet Books. p. 47.

Teach the rhyme "From Wibbleton." In *The Complete Book of Rhymes, Songs, Poems, Fingerplays, and Chants,* compiled by Jackie Silberg & Pam Schiller. 2002. Illustrated by Deborah C. Wright. Beltsville, MD: Gryphon House. p. 138.

Poem

Hoberman, Mary Ann. 1998. "Windshield Wipers." In *The Llama Who Had No Pajama.* Illustrated by Betty Fraser. San Diego: Harcourt Brace. p. 13.

Supplementary Books

Appelt, Kathi. 1996. *Watermelon Day*. Illustrated by Dale Gottlieb. New York: Henry Holt.

Cronin, Doreen. 2003. *Diary of a Worm*. Illustrated by Harry Bliss. New York: Harper-Collins.

Fleming, Candace. 2004. *Smile Lily*. Illustrated by Yumi Heo. New York: Atheneum Books for Young Readers.

Murray, Marjorie Dennis. 2003. *Don't Wake Up the Bear*. Illustrated by Patricia Wittmann. New York: Marshall Cavendish.

Peet, Bill. 1996. *The Wump World*. Boston: Houghton Mifflin.

Your Ideas

Use this space to record your own ideas for books, materials, and activities.

Y

Learning the Letter "Y"

Read Aloud

Sloat, Teri. 2000. *Farmer Brown Shears His Sheep: A Yarn about Wool.* Illustrated by Nadine Bernard Westcott. New York: DK Publishing.

☙

This rhymed text tells the yarn about sheep that were very cold after Farmer Brown sheared them. The sheep race after their fleece from stop to stop as it is carded, spun into yarn, and knitted into cardigans. The sheep are happy with their new sweaters by the yarn's end. Adult readers will get a laugh from the play on words.

Read Aloud to Emphasize the Sound of "Y"

Read aloud a second time. Words starting with "Y" are limited to "yarn" in this story.

Experience-based Chart Story: Yarn Doll

MATERIALS: Skeins of yellow yarn, 4"×6" index cards or stiff cardboard, scissors.

PROCEDURE: Engage the help of volunteers (fifth graders would be perfect) so that each child has a helper. Have the children follow these directions:

Wind the yarn around the long side of the index card about sixty times. Keep the winding loose. Slip a six-inch strand of yarn under the top section of the wound yarn. Tie the strand into a knot to secure the top. Cut the bottom of the wound yarn. Remove the index card. Tie a piece of yarn around the top one inch of the yarn figure. This step creates the doll's head. Pull away about ten strands from each side of the figure. Tie a strand of yarn at each end of these pieces to create the doll's arms and hands. Tie a piece of yarn around the middle of the yarn figure. Have the children give a name to their dolls.

After the group has gathered in front of the chart paper, ask them to recount their experiences creating yarn dolls. Be sure to add your own sentences to ensure that the letter "Y" is included. Ways to add "Y" might be: yet, yarn, yellow, yes.

As an alternative, distribute language experience paper. Have your group draw pictures about creating yarn dolls and write scribble stories. Encourage them to include whatever letters they now know how to write. Ask each individual child to dictate his or her story to a "secretary" (you, an older student, a parent, a volunteer).

Sound of the Letter Activity: Yards of Yarn Search

MATERIALS: A skein of yellow yarn, index cards, glue. From your Phonemic Awareness Picture File and other sources of pictures, such as magazines, coloring books, and phonic workbooks, find duplicate pictures of items that begin with "Y," for example, yak, yarn, yellow, yam, yard, yacht, yardstick, yarmulke, yawn, yeast, yogurt, yolk, yo-yo, yucca.

PREPARATION: For each child cut three yards of yarn. Make sets of cards for each child by gluing eight pictures to index cards, four with items that begin with "Y" and four that do not. Punch a hole in one corner of each of the cards. Thread a six-inch length or longer of yarn through the hole. Make a knot to secure. Loosely tie eight cards (four of items that begin with "Y" and four that do not) onto the three-yard length of yarn at various points. Tie a card with the child's name at one end of the three-yard length of yarn. Hide the lengths of yarn with the attached cards in various parts of the classroom or outdoors on the playground.

PROCEDURE: Tell the children to search for "Y" sounds by following the yarn with their name on it. Tell them that each time they find a "Y" sound, they should yell, "Yabba Yabba Yoo!" Have them untie and collect the cards of items that begin with "Y." When they hand in their "Y" cards, give them a piece of yellow colored candy, like lemon or pineapple hard candy.

Letter Identification Activity

MATERIALS: Tag board, yellow yarn, glue.

PROCEDURE: Have the children write a large letter "Y" on the tag board. Have them glue the yarn to the letter. Have them place this page in their key ring alphabet binder.

Play with Language

Teach and have the children sing "Yankee Doodle."

Interjections abound among words beginning with "Y." These include: yippie, yummy, yum, yesiree, yes!, yucky, yow, yup, yoo hoo, yo-heave-ho, yip, yo, yipe, yech, yadda, yadda, yadda. Your turn! What would be a fun way to use this information?

Poem

Hymes, Lucia, & James L. Jr. "My Favorite Word." In *Sing a Song of Popcorn,* selected by Beatrice Schenk de Regniers, Eva Moore, Mary Michaels White, & Jan Carr. 1988. New York: Scholastic. p. 99.

Supplementary Books

Johnston, Tony. 2003. *Go Track a Yak.* Illustrated by Tim Raglin. New York: Simon & Schuster Books for Young Readers.

Oppenheim, Shulamith Levey. 1999. *Yanni Rubbish.* Illustrated by Doug Chayka. Honesdale, PA: Boyds Mill Press.

Raschka, Christopher. 1993. *Yo! Yes!* New York: Orchard Books.

Wells, Rosemary. 1998. *Yoko.* New York: Hyperion Books for Children.

Your Ideas

Use this space to record your own ideas for books, materials, and activities.

Z

Learning the Letter "Z"

Read Aloud

Meisel, Paul. 2003. *Zara's Hats.* New York: Dutton Children's Books.

ೞ

Zara helped her father Selig the hat maker make hats. One day the hat maker ran out of the special feathers he needed. He traveled to faraway land to find them. The hat making business suffered. The empty shop window distressed Zara. So while her father was gone, Zara created fantastic hats that the ladies loved. Resourceful Zara saved the business.

Read Aloud to Emphasize the Sound of "Z"

Read aloud to emphasize the sound of "Z." In addition to Zara, words that include "Z" are Zernockel, Fezzlewort, Fuzzbottom.

Experience-based Chart Story: Cereal Box Chapeaux

MATERIALS: Chart paper, marker, empty cereal boxes, scissors, glue, construction paper, scraps of cloth, items and pictures of items that start with "Z," such as: zany (as in a clown), zap, zebra, zero, zig zag, zilch, zinnia, zip code, zoo, zipper, zucchini, zwieback, ziti. Find pictures from your Phonemic Awareness Picture File and other sources.

PREPARATION: With the help of volunteers, cut a circle in the middle of one side of each cereal box so that the box can become the basis for a hat for each child. Have the children try on their boxes and adjust them to fit their heads. Have the children decorate their hats with items and pictures of items that start with the letter "Z." Put music appropriate for a hat fashion show on the CD player. Have the children parade around the classroom to show off their creations.

After the children have gathered in front of the chart paper have them dictate a recounting of their hat making experiences. Add your own contribution to be sure "Z" words are included.

As an alternative, distribute language experience paper. Have your group draw pictures about their hat creation experiences and write scribble stories. Encourage them to include whatever letters they now know how to write. Have them dictate their scribble story to a "secretary" (you, an older student, a parent, a volunteer).

Sound of the Letter Activity: Hat Fashion Show

Have the children show off their creations. Tell the children to describe their hats by pointing out all the "Z" words with which the hat is decorated.

Letter Identification Activity

MATERIALS: Tag board, ziti, glue.
PROCEDURE: Have the child make a large letter "Z" with glue on the tag board. Have them glue pieces of ziti to the letter "Z." Have them place this page in their key ring alphabet binders.

Play with Language

Teach and have your children sing the song "Zip-A-Dee-Doo-Dah," the words for which can be accessed through the Internet at www.songofthesouth.com.

Teach and have your children sing the rhyme "Zoom, Zoom, Zoom." In *The Complete Book of Rhymes, Songs, Poems, Fingerplays, and Chants,* compiled by Jackie Silberg & Pam Schiller. 2002. Illustrated by Deborah C. Wright. Beltsville, MD: Gryphon House. p. 466.

Poem

Reeves, James. "The Grasshopper and the Bird." In *The Oxford Treasury of Children's Poems,* compiled by Michael Harrison & Christopher Stuart-Clark. 1988. New York: Oxford University Press. p.106.

Supplementary Books

Gollub, Matthew. 2000. *The Jazz Fly*. Illustrated by Karen Hanke. Santa Rosa, CA: Tortuga Press.

Howard, Arthur. 1999. *Cosmo Zooms*. San Diego: Harcourt Brace.

London, Jonathan. 1992. *Froggy Gets Dressed*. Illustrated by Frank Remkiewicz. New York: Viking Press.

Novak, Matt. 2002. *No Zombies Allowed*. New York: Atheneum Books for Young Readers.

Patterson, Brian. 2002. *Zigby Camps Out*. New York: HarperCollins.

Sadler, Marilyn. 1996. *Zenon Girl of the 21st Century*. Illustrated by Roger Bollen. New York: Simon & Schuster Books for Young Readers.

Shannon, George. 1981. *Lizard's Song*. Illustrated by Jose Aruego & Ariane Dewey. New York: Greenwillow Books.

Your Ideas

Use this space to record your own ideas for books, materials, and activities.

Index of Authors and Illustrators

Index of Titles

Index of Activities

Index of Songs, Dances, and Chants

About the Author

A graduate of Wilson College with a degree in psychology, NANCY ALLEN JURENKA continued her education at Western Connecticut University. She received her doctorate from Indiana University. Over the decades, she has taught reading and writing employing a wide variety of approaches: phonics, programmed, literature-based, whole language, language-experience, and basal reader in several of their many permutations. Reading has been a keen interest from childhood days spent in libraries savoring Raggedy Ann stories and Elsie Singmaster's Civil War novels to today's fascination with mysteries, hobbies, gardening, and politics. She is the author and co-author of four earlier books for Teacher Ideas Press: *Responding to Literature: Activities for Grades 6, 7, and 8, Beyond the Bean Seed, Cultivating a Child's Imagination Through Gardening,* and *Hobbies Through Children's Books and Activities.* She believes that successful literacy development must be based upon real experiences combined with captivating children's books. She teaches children's literature and reading education courses at Central Washington University.